LITERARY CRITICISM AND THEORY

COVERS ALL IMPORTANT TOPICS AND PREVIOUS YEARS' QUESTION PAPERS

RACHANA AMARNATH

Contents

Contents

Preface

This book, Literary criticism and theory, is well researched, detailed, and critically analytical in its approach.

The book is guided by its uniquity teaching attempt that is to combine each topic with video leactures, which can be access via scanning the QR code.

It will not only enhance the reading of the texts but also intrigue the learners to delve into the world of literature. Literature has the ability to transport its readers into a world of fantasy,fiction and imagination. We can explore and go beyond boundaries, appreciate the beauty of nature, reach the unreachable, achieve the unachievable. Prose and Poetry has an indelible and lasting impact on human mind. Through this book we aim to develop this into our readers. We wish to take our reader to a world where they can enjoy and appreciate literature, critically analyse poetry and understand the poets or the author's point of view. One can get a glimpse into that era , those times and the life of a particular time period, thus getting a peek into the writer's world and his mind.

The book aims to provide an enriching experience , which can help us enhance various realms of life.the book will also provide excellence material, critical analysis and information that will provide growth to its readers and enjoyment at the same time.

I

Introduction of Literary criticism & Theory

Literary criticism (or literary studies) is the study, evaluation, and interpretation of literature. Modern literary criticism is often influenced by literary theory, which is the philosophical discussion of literature's goals and methods. Though the two activities are closely related, literary critics are not always, and have not always been, theorists.

In other words, "Literary criticism" refers to the act of interpreting and studying literature. A literary critic is not someone who merely evaluates the worth or quality of a piece of literature but, rather, is someone who argues on behalf of an interpretation or understanding of the particular meaning(s) of literary texts. The task of a literary critic is to explain and attempt to reach a critical understanding of what literary texts mean in terms of their aesthetic, as well as social, political, and cultural statements and suggestions. A literary critic does more than simply discuss or evaluate the importance of a literary text; rather, a literary critic seeks to reach a logical and reasonable understanding of not only what a text's author intends for it to mean but, also, what different cultures and ideologies render it capable of meaning.

"Literary theory," refers to a particular form of literary criticism in which particular academic, scientific, or philosophical approaches are followed in a systematic fashion while analyzing literary texts. For example, a psychoanalytic theorist might examine and interpret a literary text strictly through the theoretical lens of psychoanalysis and psychology and, in turn, offer an interpretation or reading of a text that focuses entirely on the psychological dimensions of it. Traditional literary criticism tends not to focus on a particular aspect of (or approach to) a literary text in quite the same manner that literary theory usually does. Literary theory proposes particular, systematic approaches to literary texts that impose a particular line of intellectual reasoning to it.

Block- 1 Indian Aesthetics.

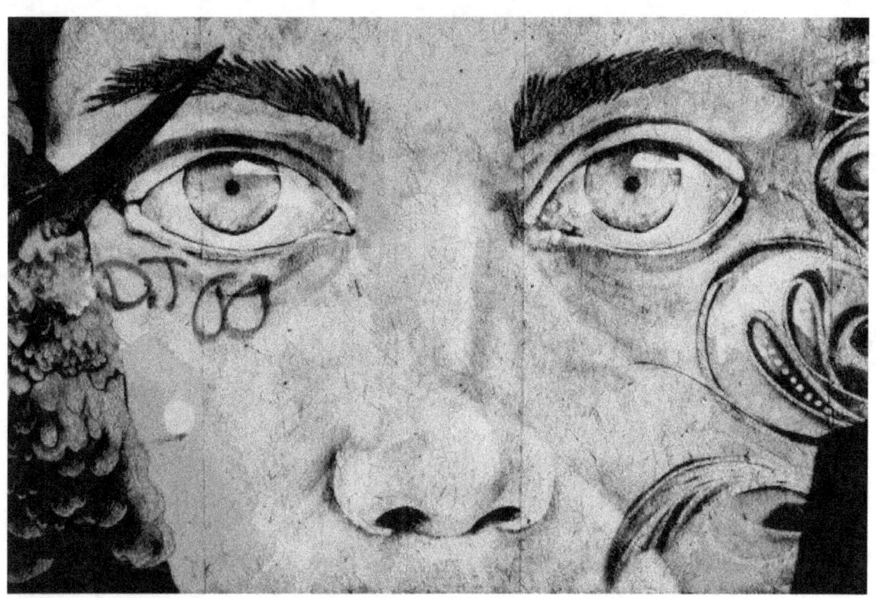

Introduction

Indian aesthetics is a unique philosophical and spiritual point of view on art, architecture and literature. The word "aesthetics" belongs to the field of the science and philosophy of fine art. Fine art has the capacity to present the "Absolute" in sensuous garb and aesthetic relation. Indian aesthetics is primarily concerned with three arts—poetry, music, and architecture—however, sculpture and painting are also studied under aesthetic theories.

Indian art evolved with an emphasis on inducing special spiritual or philosophical states in the audience, or with representing them symbolically. Of particular concern to Indian drama and literature are the term 'bhava' or the state of mind and rasa referring generally to the emotional flavors/essence crafted into the work by the writer and relished by a 'sensitive spectator' or one with positive taste and mind.

II
Rasa Theory

Scan for the video

Bharat Muni

- In Indian aesthetics, a rasa literally means "nectar, essence or taste". It connotes a concept in Indian arts about the aesthetic flavor of any visual, literary or musical work that evokes an emotion or feeling in the reader or audience but cannot be described.

- Rasa Theory asserts that entertainment (music poetry, drama, performance) is expected to evoke Rasa or joy, but that is not the primary goal. The primary goal is instead to create parallel life in front of the audience to experience a sense of one's own.

- The theory of rasa is attributed to Bharata, a sage-priest who may have lived sometime between the 1st century BCE and the 3rd century CE.

- It was developed by the rhetorician and philosopher Abhinavagupta (c. 1000), who applied it to all varieties of theatre and poetry.

- The principal human feelings, according to Bharata, are delight, laughter, sorrow, anger, energy, fear, disgust, heroism, and astonishment, all of which may be recast in contemplative form as the various rasas: erotic, comic, pathetic, furious, heroic, terrible, odious, marvelous, and quietistic. These rasas comprise the components of aesthetic experience. The power to taste rasa is a reward for merit in some previous existence.

Features of Rasa Theory

1. Rasa means aesthetics, juice, essence, taste in performance.
2. Rasa is an undefinable realization and intense feelings with detachment.
3. It is the flavor (general) or aesthetic emotion (metaphorical).
4. It is the soul of poetry.
5. Rasa is an emotion and cannot be described in opposition to Aristotle.
6. Originally, Rasa means juice, essence.
7. It is the pleasure experienced by each class of people.
8. No other word can define Rasa completely.
9. It is the impression created on the mind of the sympathetic audience by the expressions of Bhavas (emotions) and it's experienced by it.
10. Rasa is not experienced in common situations but only in the art form.

Conclusion:

In the Indian performing arts, a rasa is an emotion inspired in an audience by a performer. They are described by Bharata Muni in the Nātyasāstra, an ancient work of dramatic theory. Rasas are created by bhavas: the gestures and facial expressions of the actors. Expressing Rasa in classical Indian dance form is referred to as Rasa-abhinaya. The Nātyasāstra carefully delineates the bhavas used to create each rasa.

The theory of rasas still forms the aesthetic underpinning of all Indian classical dance and theatre, such as Bharatanatyam, kathak, Kuchipudi, Odissi, Manipuri, Kudiyattam, Kathakali and others.

III

Dhvani Theory

Scan for the video

Anandavardhana

- The theory of Dhvani in the field of rhetoric and aesthetics being put forward by Ānandavardhana through his monumental work Dhvanyāloka. It is a contribution of Sanskrit to the universal poetic aesthetic studies.
- The word Dhvani literally means "sound", but in theory it does not deal with the function of sound in the musical sense.
- The Dhvani theory considers the indirectly evoked meaning or suggestivity as the characteristic features of literary utterance.
- In his work Dhvanyaloka, Anandavardhana establishes his theory that suggestion is the soul of poetry. He says that beautiful ideas in poetry are of two kinds

1) literal meaning (Vacya) and
2) Implied i.e., suggestive meaning (pratiyamana)

This implied sense is something more than the literal meaning and depends of the whole poem and not merely on its parts. The expressed sense is invariably an idea or a figure of speech but the suggested sense may be of three kinds

1) an idea(vastudvani)
2) a figure of speech(alankaradvani) or an

3) emotion(rasadvani)

Such poetry in which the words and their literal meanings occupy a subordinate position and suggest some charming sense is called dhvani. It is the highest type of poetry.

- Anandavardhana uses the term dhvani to designate the universe of suggestion. (The soul of kavya is dhvani, he says).
- Anandavardhana integrates the theory ofthe rasa with his dhvani theory; that is, he t says that dhvani is the method through which the effect of rasa is achieved. Rasa is the effect of suggestion.

IV
Sphota Theory

Scan for the video

- Sphoṭa ("bursting, opening", "spurt") is an important concept in the Indian grammatical tradition of Vyakarana, relating to the problem of speech production, how the mind orders linguistic units into coherent discourse and meaning.
- The theory of sphoṭa is associated with Bhartṛhari (c. 5th century[1]), an early figure in Indic linguistic theory, mentioned in the 670s by Chinese traveler Yijing. Bhartṛhari is the author of the Vākyapadīya. His work Vakyapadiya was based on Grammar.
- Sphoṭa, literally means "sudden opening", "disclosure", it is taking place in both speaker and hearer, through the process of articulation in both.
- Bhratrihari says in his treatise, Vakyapcrdiya, that what communicates the meaning of a word or sentence is technical called sphota.

It is of three kinds:-

i) Varnasphota i.e. the sphota of Varna which literally means the alphabet; so that Varnasphota is a reference to the meaning of letters.

ii) Padasphota: sphota of padas. That is the meaning of words.

iii) Vakyasphota : the meaning vakya that is sentence.

The differentiation between sound and articulation is one of the fundamental features of the theory of Sphoṭa. Sphota is not a sound we hear but the sound we articulate.

- Bhartrahari's view is that meaning is not conveyed from the speaker to the listener , rather the spoken words serves only stimulus to reveal or uncover the meaning, which was already present in the mind of the listener or hearer.
- It pertains to the problem of articulation of speech and how the mind arranges linguistic units into meaning and ultimately discourses.

Bhartrahari theorized the act of speech as being made up of three stages:

1. Conceptualization by the speaker (ideas)
2. Performance of speaking (Madhyama -Medium)
3. Comprehension by the interpreter (Vaikhari- complete utterance)

V
Auchitya Theory

Scan for the video

- Among the numerous schools of Sanskrit poetics Aucitya is another important school. Aucitya means poetic harmony. In the Aucityavicāracarcā, Kṣmendra puts forwards the novel doctrine of Aucitya (Propriety or appropriateness) is the soul of poetry. Kṣmendra is known as the founder of Aucitya School in Sanskrit poetics.
- Auchitya is a Hindi word taken from Sanskrit. It means justification, propriety, decency.
- Propriety can be defined in this context as the details or rules of behavior conventionally considered to be correct. Or that which is correct, appropriate, and fitting. The word Auchitya also contains the Hindi word "Uchit" which in English means "appropriate".

- A poem is a collection of words used to describe ideas or emotions in a vivid and imaginative style. The Auchitya can be described as the alphabet used to do that.
- This is the only theory that is accepted by all the poets without any arguments. Thus, it is also called the "Theory of coordination" because it regulates all the constituents of the Natya Shastra.

- To use the elements of a poem such that they deliver essence in their appropriate place is called "Auchitya". For example, to use Rasa, Alankara, Riti, etc. in an appropriate place is Auchitya. The poem should explain or incorporate a Rasa wherever needed else it loses its beauty.

Features of Auchitya

- It is the only element that includes Guna, Dosha, Alamkara, Dhavani, Rasa, and Vakrata.
- Includes both types of poems i.e. Bahva and Rupa.
- It is independent of the reader's interest.
- It is as important for a poem as values are in our life.

Types of Auchitya By Kshemendra

1. Pada (Phrase)
2. Vakya(sentence)
3. Prabhandhanartha (the meaning of the whole composition)
4. Guna(qualities)
5. Alankara(poetic figure)
6. Rasa (State of being)
7. Kriya(Verb)
8. Karaka (case ending)
9. Linga(Gender)
10. Vachana (Number)
11. Visheshana (Qualification)
12. Upsarga (Prefix)
13. Nipata (Redundancies)
14. Kala (Time)
15. Desh (country)
16. Kula (Family)

17. Vrata (custom)
18. Tatva (Truth)
19. Satva(Inherent self)
20. Abhipraya (Motive)
21. Swabhava (Nature)
22. Sarsangraha (essential property)
23. Pratibha (Innate ability)
24. Avastha (state)
25. Vichara(Thought)
26. Nama(Name)
27. Aashirwada(Blessings)

Conclusion

Emotions are an integral part of humans. Many times words are not sufficient to describe everything. This is where Auchitya comes into the picture enabling the writers/authors to silently nudge the readers towards the direction they want us to stir in.

VI

Alamkara Theory

Scan for the video

- Alamkara, also referred to as palta or alankaram, is a concept in Indian classical music and literally means "ornament, decoration".

- Basically this is a study of language. If you have studied the grammar of any Indian language, you must have come across repeated use of this word, which literally means "ornament". But, of course, alamkara is not mere decorative poetry, or embellishments in literature. The alamkaras are various figures of speech but with these latter are models of how meaning is or ought to be apprehended.

- Bahama,Dandin, and Udbhata of the sixth, seventh, and ninth centuries respectively have all talked about this literary device. The first among them, Bahama, talks of the pleasure of muitiplicity of meaning inherent in certain alamkaras such as samasokti.

- The theory of alankara seems to have influenced poetic compositions in Sanskrit. Though the theory of alankaras was the oldest in literary speculation, and was superseded by theories of rasa and dhvani. Yet alankara was a subject dealt with even by the writers of comparatively recent times. For example, Mammata and Visvanatha, though they were followers of the rasa-dhavani theory, have devoted considerable space to alamkaras. This would convey an idea of the extent of the influence that the alankara school exerted on poetry as well as on the theory of poetry.

- As the tradition was developed, Anandavardhana sought to integrate with dhvani and rasa. Dhvani is evoked by figures of speech (alamkara). And as we have already seen, the former leads to an evocation of rasa. Some theorists have categorized alamkara as both phonetic-based and meaning-based: sabdaalamkara and arthalamkara. Though these are two main categories, there are numerous subcategories into which alamkara has been divided.

1) Sadmsya(similarity)
2) Virodha (opposition)
3) Smkhalabadha (chain bound)
4) Tarka nyaya (reasoning logic),
5) Lokanyaya (popular logic)
6) Kavyanyaya Oogic of poetry)
7) Gudharatha pratiti (interference of meaning)
Mammata enumerates sixty-one figures and groups them into seven types:
1) upama (simile)
2) rupaku (metaphor)
3) aprastuta prasamsa (indirect description)
4) dipaka (stringed figures)
5) vyatireka (dissimilitude)
6) virodha (contradiction)
7) samuccaya (concatenation)

Block-2 Classical Criticism

What is Classicism?

Classicism, in the arts, refers generally to a high regard for a classical period, classical antiquity in the Western tradition, as setting standards for taste which the classicists seek to emulate. In its purest form, classicism is an aesthetic attitude dependent on principles based in the culture, art and literature of ancient Greece and Rome, with the emphasis on form, simplicity proportion, clarity of structure, perfection, restrained emotion, as well as explicit appeal to the intellect.

What is Classical Criticism?

Classical literary criticism and its theories can be traced to classical Greek and Roman philosophy. Greek philosopher Plato's literary theory can be found in his ten-volume Republic, in which he discusses the concept of mimesis and argues that art, and therefore literature, can only imitate the physical world, and the physical world itself is but an imitation of the world of ideas. To Plato, art serves no purpose, it has no useful role in life, because it doesn't represent true reality and is therefore corrupt and is meant only for pleasure, the latter of which Plato eschewed.

In his famous Poetics, Greek philosopher Aristotle argues that art and literature may be a form of mimesis but is at the same time a natural form of expression. He posits that imagination is a part of art and a component of imitation that promotes the "manipulation of ideas" and that it can expose truths that are related to human nature. Aristotle views poetry, therefore, as philosophical and a part of conceptualizing the things that can happen in life, but not necessarily imitating or mimicking something directly.

Aristotle also discusses the concept of "Organic Unity," which argues that good artistic expression is made up of many parts that work together in unity to create the work of art. If there is a missing part, the art won't be good art and will not serve a purpose.

A final example of classical literary criticism comes from Roman philosopher Horace, who, in his Ars Poetica: Epistle to the Pisos, argues that poetry can be enjoyable and still have a functional purpose. He believed that poetry can be used as a teaching tool, while at the same time providing a pleasurable experience.

VII
Plato on Imitation and Art

Plato

Introduction: Plato was an ancient Greek philosopher born in Athens during the Classical period in Ancient Greece. In Athens, Plato founded the Academy, a philosophical school where he taught the philosophical doctrines that would later become known as Platonism.

Platonic criticism, literary criticism based on the philosophical writings of Plato, especially his views on art expressed in Phaedrus, Ion, and the Republic. In practice Platonic criticism is part of an extensive approach to literature, involving an examination of the moral, ethical, and historical effects of a work of art.

For Plato, the visual world was an imitation of the ideal forms, which alone were real. Art, therefore, was no more than an imitation of an imitation and of value only insofar as it directed the soul toward the real—i.e., Truth, Beauty, or the Good.

Plato's Objection on Poetry

Scan for the video

Q.1 Why does Plato declare the role of the poet as subversive? Explain.
or
Bring out the salient features of Plato's attack on poetry.
Ans.

Introduction: Plato was an ancient Greek philosopher born in Athens during the Classical period in Ancient Greece. Platonic criticism, literary criticism based on the philosophical writings of Plato, especially his views on art expressed in Phaedrus, Ion, and the Republic. For Plato, the visual world was an imitation of the ideal forms, which alone were real. Art, therefore, was no more than an imitation of an imitation and of value only insofar as it directed the soul toward the real—i.e., Truth, Beauty, or the Good.

Plato's view on Poetry.

Plato was opposed to poetry. In particular, he did not like the mimetic aspect of poetry – namely that poetry imitated life. This aspect of poetry was seen as opposed to true reality. Plato had a robust idea that what one really needed to know was the eternal forms and one could only gain this knowledge through dialectics, that is, philosophy. This is why Plato banished the poets from

his ideal Republic. However, to say that Plato does not use poetry in his writings would be wrong. Any platonic scholar would tell you that Plato uses plenty of poetic forms and devices all throughout his works. I think he does this, because he sees himself as a true philosopher. True philosophers are not really prone to the dangers of poetry, because they have been trained in the school of philosophy.

As a moralist, Plato disapproves of poetry because it is immoral, as a philosopher he disapproves of it because it is based in falsehood. He is of the view that philosophy is better than poetry because philosopher deals with idea / truth, whereas poet deals with what appears to him. He believed that truth of philosophy was more important than the pleasure of poetry. He argued that most of it should be banned from the ideal society that he described in the Republic.

Plato's objection to Poetry from the point of view of Education:

a. In 'The Republic' Book II – He condemns poetry as fostering evil habits and vices in children. Homer's epics were part of studies. Heroes of epics were not examples of sound or ideal morality. They were lusty, cunning, and cruel – war mongers. Even Gods were no better.

b. Plato writes: "if we mean our future guardians to regard the habit of quarreling among themselves as of all things the basest, no word should be said to them of the wars in the heaven, or of the plots and fighting of the gods against one another, for they are not true.... If they would only believe as we would tell them that quarreling is unholy, and that never up to this time has there been any quarreling between citizens...... these tales (of epics) must not be admitted into our State, whether they are supposed to have allegorical meaning or not."

c. Thus he objected on the ground that poetry does not cultivate good habits among children

Objection from Philosophical point of view:

a. In 'The Republic' Book X: Poetry does not lead to, but drives us away form the realization of the ultimate reality – the Truth.

b. Philosophy is better than poetry because Philosophy deals with idea and poetry is twice removed from original idea.

c. Plato says: "The imitator or maker of the image knows nothing of true existence; he knows appearance only. The imitative art is an inferior who marries an inferior and has inferior offspring.

Objection form the Moral point of view:

a. In the same book 'The Republic': Soul of man has higher principles of reason as well as lower constituted of baser impulses and emotions. Whatever encourages and strengthens the rational principle is good, and emotional is bad.

b. Poetry waters and nourishes the baser impulses of men - emotional, sentimental and sorrowful. Plato says: "Then the imitative poet who aims at being popular is not by nature made, nor is his art intended, to please or to affect the rational principle in the soul; but he will prefer the passionate and fitful temper, which is easily limited .... And therefore, we shall be right in refusing to admit him into a well-ordered state, because he awakens and nourishes and strengthen the feelings and impairs the reason. Poetry feeds and waters the passion instead of drying them up; she lets them rule, although they ought to be controlled, if mankind are ever to increase in happiness and virtue."

Conclusion:

In Plato's opinion, poetry cannot shape the character of the individual not can it promote the well-being of the state. It is a copy of the copy. It is twice removed from reality. He condemns poetry on three grounds.

1. Poetic inspiration
2. The emotional appeal of poetry
3. Its non-moral character.

Plato's view on Mimeses (Imitation)

Scan for the video

Q.1 Short note on Mimeses

Or

Q.1 Explain Plato's view of art as imitation.

Ans.

Introduction: Plato was an ancient Greek philosopher born in Athens during the Classical period in Ancient Greece. Platonic criticism, literary criticism based on the philosophical writings of Plato, especially his views on art expressed in Phaedrus, Ion, and the Republic. For Plato, the visual world was an imitation of the ideal forms, which alone were real. Art, therefore, was no more than an imitation of an imitation and of value only insofar as it directed the soul toward the real—i.e., Truth, Beauty, or the Good.

Plato's view on mimeses.

- In Greek, mimesis means "imitation" not in the sense of "copying" but in the sense of "representation". According to Plato and Aristotle, mimesis is the imitation of nature. Plato states that all artistic creations are forms of imitations that exist in the "world of ideas" and created by God. The material things that are perceived are representations of the ideal type or observable reality.
- In the theory of mimesis, Plato claims that art is imitated by nature, an imitation of life. He says that the "idea" is the reality. Thus, imitation of reality is the art of imitating the idea.
- His famous example of a carpenter and a chair explains his beliefs better. First, the idea of the chair comes to the carpenter's mind, then the carpenter gives the chair a physical shape, he ends up creating his idea, the chair. Hence, the carpenter's chair is being removed from reality, twice.
- He thinks that philosophy is more important than poetry because philosophy deals with ideas whereas poetry deals with illusion. For Plato, the poet's imitation is removed from reality twice so their creations are unreal and illusion of truth. Poetry is mimetic as philosophy is, but Plato denies poetry because it is only mimetic in philosophical and moral grounds, meaning that imitation of poetry can make the best men feel sad, sorrowful, and depressed.

· Some can say that it is normal, but in those times, the stated feelings were feminine and were not appropriate for men being sentimental. Also, Plato says that poets can depict the gods in inappropriate ways.

VIII
Aristotle theory of Imitation and Tragedy

Aristotle

Q.1 Explain and discuss Aristotle's view of literature as imitation.

Ans.

Introduction:

Aristotle (384-322 BC) was an eminent Greek philosopher. He was also devoted to many branches of knowledge like mathematics, political philosophy, natural science and the Arts. In his Poetics, Aristotle addresses many problems that Plato had raised, about the function and nature of poetry. Rhetoric and Poetics contain the bulk of literary criticism of Aristotle and both were his lecture notes. Poetics raises many important critical issues constantly debated by scholars. Poetics also made terms like mimesis, catharsis, hamartia and hubris popular in literary criticism.

Aristotle's Views on Imitation (Mimesis)

Scan for the video

Aristotle's Poetics is particularly concerned with mimesis, a Greek word used within literary theory and philosophy that loosely translates to "representation" or "imitation." In Ancient Greece, where Aristotle lived and wrote, art—including visual art and poetry—was considered mimetic. This idea means that, in one way or another, all art is a representation or imitation of nature, including human nature.

Mimesis was a hot topic in Aristotle's time, and some writers and philosophers, such as Plato in his work The Republic, warned that art, especially poetry, should be approached with caution, as it is merely an imitation of nature as created in God's vision.

In Poetics, Aristotle upholds the popular belief that all poetry is a form of mimesis; however, he implies that imitation isn't necessarily a bad thing, in large part because all human beings are naturally prone to imitation and respond to it with pleasure.

Aristotle argues that all forms of poetry—tragedy, epic poetry, comedy, dithyrambic poetry and dance; and music performed by pipe or lyre—are forms of imitation and can only differ three ways: their medium, their object, and their mode of imitation.

In all poetry, Aristotle says, "the medium of imitation is rhythm, language and melody," and different types of poetic expression employ these mediums separately or together in some combination. For instance, music may use melody and rhythm, whereas dance uses only rhythm and tragedy uses all three. Imitations must have an object, and poetry imitates "agents," meaning people and events. These objects "must be either admirable or inferior," and the difference, Aristotle argues, is the difference between a tragedy and a comedy.

Imitation is accomplished in Homer's Odyssey, an epic poem, through the narration of a single person. In other forms of poetry, like tragic plays, imitation is created through multiple agents engaged in some activity. Poetry as a form of artistic expression can vary in many ways; however, Aristotle maintains that all poetry is a form of imitation.

According to Aristotle, "imitation comes naturally to human beings from childhood." This is how humans are different from animals, Aristotle says, as people learn through imitation and have a strong inclination to imitate people and things.

Conclusion: For Aristotle, imitation is not a question of good or bad, as it is for Plato; imitation, and therefore the creation of art and poetry, is simply human nature and will always be a part of the human experience. Aristotle maintains that some imitation is bad, such as a poorly-written poem that ignores probability or necessity, or a badly executed painting in which a female deer is depicted with antlers (because only male deer have antlers). But for Aristotle, the fact that some imitations are bad doesn't mean that all imitations are bad. While Aristotle doesn't explicitly state whether imitation and therefore poetry is good or bad, he does imply that its existence is inevitable and should be assessed and questioned more thoroughly.

Aristotle's view of 'Catharsis

Scan for the video

Q. 2 Discuss Aristotle's view of 'Catharsis'.

Introduction: Aristotle (384-322 BC) was an eminent Greek philosopher. He was also devoted to many branches of knowledge like mathematics, political philosophy, natural science and the Arts. In his Poetics, Aristotle addresses many problems that Plato had raised, about the function and nature of poetry. Rhetoric and Poetics contain the bulk of literary criticism of Aristotle and both were his lecture notes. Poetics raises many important critical issues constantly debated by scholars. Poetics also made terms like mimesis, catharsis, hamartia and hubris popular in literary criticism.

Concept of Catharsis:

- The process of expressing strong feeling, for example through plays or other artistic activities, as a way of getting rid of anger, reducing suffering, etc. In other words, catharsis means, the purification or purgation of the emotions (especially pity and fear) primarily through art.

- In criticism, catharsis is a metaphor used by Aristotle in the Poetics to describe the effects of true tragedy on the spectator. The use is derived from the medical term katharsis (Greek: "purgation" or "purification"). Aristotle states that the purpose of tragedy is to arouse "terror and pity" and thereby effect the catharsis of these emotions. His exact meaning has been the subject of critical debate over the centuries.

- In criticism, catharsis is a metaphor used by Aristotle in the Poetics to describe the <u>effects of true tragedy on the spectator.</u> The use is derived from the medical term katharsis (Greek: "purgation" or "purification"). Aristotle states that the purpose of tragedy is <u>to arouse "terror and pity"</u> and thereby effect the catharsis of these emotions. His exact meaning has been the subject of critical debate over the centuries.

- Aristotle's use of the word catharsis is not a technical reference to purgation or purification but a beautiful metaphor for the peculiar tragic pleasure, the feeling of being washed or cleansed.

- Aristotle states that the purpose of tragedy is to arouse "terror and pity" and thereby effect the catharsis of these emotions.

- Scholars and critics interested in the study of tragedy have always been attracted to the concept of "Catharsis". Indeed Catharsis is one of the most celebrated terms in the field of literary criticism.

- On the basis of understanding its usage in Aristotle's Poetics and his other work, such as Politics and Ethics , critics have attempted to explain this term. They have advanced three different meanings to the term 'Catharsis': 'purgation' or 'purification' or 'clarification'.

- Though the critics have differed in their interpretation of this term, however, they have agreed upon the fact that tragedy arouses 'pity' and 'fear' which lead to 'tragic pleasure'.

Q.3 Write short note on Hamartia.
Definition:
The term hamartia derives from the Greek hamartánein, which means <u>"to miss the mark" or "to err"</u>. It is most often associated with Greek tragedy, although it is also used in Christian theology. The term is often said to depict the flaws or defects of a character and portraying these as the reason of a potential downfall. In other words, Hamartia is a literary term that refers to a tragic flaw or error that leads to a character's downfall.

The concept of hamartia first appears in Aristotle's Poetics, the earliest known work of dramatic theory, written in 335 BCE.

Aristotle argued that a good tragedy is neither about the downfall of a great man nor the success of a villain, but about the demise of someone who is simply human—neither evil nor a model of virtue—and, in that regard, relatable to the audience. But to be human is to be flawed, Aristotle points out. Therefore, he argues, tragedies should tell the story of someone whose downfall is caused not by greed or vice, but "by some error or frailty." This, according to Aristotle, is hamartia.

Although hamartia can be found in many works that do not align with Aristotle's definition of tragedy, it's important to note that only works that have tragic heroes (or, protagonists whose actions lead to their own downfall) can be said to contain examples of hamartia. Especially in classical tragedies, hubris (or excessive self-confidence) is a common trait that exemplifies hamartia.

Q.4 Discuss Aristotle's view on Tragedy?

Introduction:

Aristotle (384-322 BC) was an eminent Greek philosopher. He was also devoted to many branches of knowledge like mathematics, political philosophy, natural science and the Arts. In his Poetics, Aristotle addresses many problems that Plato had raised, about the function and nature of poetry. Rhetoric and Poetics contain the bulk of literary criticism of Aristotle and both were his lecture notes. Poetics raises many important critical issues constantly debated by scholars. Poetics also made terms like mimesis, catharsis, hamartia and hubris popular in literary criticism.

The centre piece of Aristotle's Poetics is his examination of tragedy. Aristotle defines tragedy, explains its constituent parts and compares it with epic. He writes:

Tragedy, then, is an imitation of an action that is serious, complete, and of a certain magnitude; in language embellished with each kind of artistic ornament, the several kinds being found in separate parts of the play; in the form of action, not of narrative; through pity and fear effecting the proper catharsis of these emotions.

Features of tragedy:

Aristotle indicates that the medium of tragedy is drama and not narrative. He says that tragedy "shows" rather than "tells". According to him tragedy is higher and more philosophical than history because history simply relates what has happened while tragedy dramatizes what may happen, "what is possible according to the law of probability or necessity." He says that history deals with the particular and tragedy with the universal. Real events that have happened may be due to accident or coincidence and they may not be a part of a clear cause-effect chain. Therefore, they have little relevance for others. Tragedy, on the other hand, is rooted in the fundamental order of the universe and it creates a cause-

and-effect chain that clearly reveals what may happen at any time or place because that is the way the world operates. Tragedy therefore arouses not only pity but also fear, because the audience can place themselves within this cause-and-effect chain.

Importance of plots in tragedy:

Aristotle considers plot as the first principle and the most important feature of tragedy. He defines plot as the "arrangement of incidents". He implies that plot is not just the story but the way incidents are presented to the audience. According to him, the outcome of the tragedy depends on a tightly constructed cause and effect chain of actions. He also considers that plot to be more important than the character and personality of the protagonist. Aristotle also considers the ideal structure of a good plot. He says that the plot must be a whole with a beginning, middle and end. The beginning is described as the starting point of the cause-and-effect chain. The middle is caused by earlier incidents and itself becomes the cause of incidents that follow it. The end must be caused by the preceding events and should resolve the problems created during the first two stages.

Characters: Aristotle also theorizes on the character in a tragedy. He indicates that the character must be good. He also implies that character must be appropriate, the right type, i.e. a man should be brave and a woman should not necessarily be brave but neither she should be unscrupulously clever. Aristotle, further, insists that character must be consistent and he says that the poet should aim at either the necessary or the probable so that the character will be credible. He says that the poet should not only preserve the type of character but also ennoble it.

Thought:Another segment of Aristotle's view on tragedy is on thought. Aristotle maintains that thought consists of every effect that has to be produced by speech, proof, refutation, excitation of the feelings or suggestion of importance. For him, thought is one of the causes of action and it covers mind's activities from reasoning, perception and formulation of emotion. He further states that thought is expressed in speeches in a tragedy and is therefore closely linked to diction.

Diction: Diction is one of the elements in Aristotle's perception of tragedy. Diction covers language and its use: the way command, request, prayer, statement or question is expressed. Aristotle evokes the study of rhetoric in the context of diction and proposes analysis of words, sentence, letter, syllable, inflection and phrase. Further, he examines metaphors such as the metaphors of light and darkness in Oedipus Tyrannus. He also

examines lyric poetry as it is seen in choral odes.

Song and Spectacle:Aristotle indicates that song and spectacle are the elements concerned with the production of the play. Though they are essential parts of tragedy, the concern of the poet is less for them compared to his concern for plot, character and thought. Aristotle considers chorus as a device that upholds both song and spectacle. He also maintains that the chorus should be regarded as one of the actors and even of greater importance as the chorus has a unifying function in a tragedy.

Block -3 Romantic Criticism

Romanticism of the 19th century was a continental movement and English Romantic Revival can be considered as a part of European Romanticism. The distinction between the Romantic and the Classical was first explained by Schlegel. Concepts such as truth, nature, God and creativity were the important subjects in the Romantic Era. The domain of literary criticism too underwent changes so as to accommodate new approaches to art and literature.

IX
Introduction to Romanticism

• Romantic Criticism was shaped by the experience of the French Revolution and hence one of its major concerns was how literature should relate to society. This question weighed heavily with William Wordsworth, whose "Preface to Lyrical Ballads" carry the first substantial statements of Romantic Critical principles. Wordsworth spoke about the language of poetry and he maintained that the language of poetry should be democratized.

• Samuel Taylor Coleridge, on the other hand, was widely read in contemporary German philosophy. Coleridge was involved, in his Biographia Literaria to establish the principles of writing. He also made an attempt to define imagination and his interest in the power of imagination marked an important aspect of Romantic critical thinking. Reality, imagination, fancy and aesthetics were the key concepts put in circulation by Romantic Criticism.

• English poets like William Wordsworth, S.T. Coleridge and P.B. Shelley gave memorable expressions to the Romantic mindset developed by their German contemporaries. They underscored in their writings the primacy of feeling, love and pleasure, and imagination over reason. They were also convinced of the spiritual superiority of nature's organic forms over mechanical ingenuity; and of the ability of art to restore lost harmony between the individual and nature.

• Romantic Criticism, especially that of Wordsworth, made certain proclamations about the nature and function of poetry. Wordsworth's famous statement of poetry as the spontaneous overflow of powerful feelings posited a different view of poetry than was accepted at that time. Wordsworth shifted the centre of attention from the work as a reflection or imitation of reality to the artist.

• For the first time, poetry was considered an expressive rather than mimetic art. Additionally, music replaced painting as the art form considered most like poetry. In addition to the significance of poet's personality in poetry, romantic critics formulated a few aesthetic theories.

• Wordsworth's notion of poetic language in "Preface to Lyrical Ballads" and Coleridge's idea of meter in Biographia Literaria are good examples of such theories. However, Coleridge's critical theory differed widely from that of Wordsworth in that they were heavily grounded in theology. Further, Coleridge was more systematic and analytical in his critical writings.

X

'Preface' to the Lyrical Ballads by William Wordsworth

Scan for the video

William Wordsworth

Q.1 Examine Wordsworth's view that "all good poetry is the spontaneous overflow of powerful feelings."

Or

Briefly outline Wordsworth's theory of poetic diction with special reference to the 'Preface' to the Lyrical Ballads.

Or

Consider Wordsworth's 'Preface to Lyrical Ballads' as the manifesto of Romantic Literature.

Ans.

Introduction:

Preface to Lyrical Ballads is a critical statement written by William Wordsworth, who wanted to free poetry from artificial style of writing and bring it nearer to life, to the common people. The high priest of Nature, William Wordsworth was the harbinger of Romanticism in the eighteenth century.

The publication of the Lyrical Ballads, a joint venture by Wordsworth and Coleridge is a milestone in the history of literature.

The Lyrical Ballads was a collection of poems and it was published in the year 1798 under the title, Lyrical Ballads.

1. The Preface to Lyrical Ballads is an essay, composed by William Wordsworth, it has come to be seen as manifesto of the Romantic movement.

The four guidelines of the manifesto include:

- Ordinary life is the best subject for poetry. (Wordsworth uses common man's language.)
- Everyday language is best suited for poetry.
- Expression of feeling is more important than action or plot.
- "Poetry is the spontaneous overflow of emotion" that "takes its origin from emotion, recollected in tranquility."

1. The subject matter of the preface can be discussed under four heads.

a. What is poetry?
b. What are the defining characteristics of a poet?
c. The value of poetry.
d. The question of poetic diction.

a. **Defining poetry:**

"Poetry is spontaneous overflow of powerful emotion or feelings", "it takes its origin from "emotion recollected in tranquility".

When Wordsworth says that poetry is the "spontaneous overflow of powerful feelings" it is clear that poetry is a matter of mood and inspiration. Poetry evolves from the feelings of the poet. There is spontaneity in the expression of the feelings. Powerful feelings and emotions are fundamental, without them great poetry cannot be written.

In tranquility, he recalls his emotions. The emotions are made into a poem with the help of images of those things in nature which aroused the poet's emotion.

b. **The Poet's Characteristics:**

- First, he should to be exceptionally sensitive and more comprehensive soul than are supposed to be common among mankind.

- Secondly, he should be a man speaking to man that is to say poetry is not mere self-indulgence and that the poet is a social being with a responsibility.
- Thirdly, the poet should endowed with an extraordinarily strong imagination so that he is affected by absent things as if they were present.

c. The Value of Poetry.

- The universal function of poetry is to make readers sensitive and human.
- Poetry does not merely leave provide pleasure, but teachers moral and philosophical values to readers.
- Poetry can refine and regenerate mankind.
- Poetry is the image of man and nature.
- William Wordsworth believe that every poet has the social responsibility of strengthening and promoting human culture through his poetry.

d. Poetic Diction (Language)

- The poetic diction is the essay as suggested by Wordsworth applies that "real language of men". He has selected it to communicate and connect it with the other man and common people.
- He further at that the selection of the common language can add "vivid sensation and pleasure" as each and every poem has its own "purpose to share and evoke" pleasure to the readers.
- Wordsworth criticized new classical writer such as Dryden and Pop for using artificial poetic language.
- He believed that figure of speech should be organic to a poem. They should not be added like ornaments.

Conclusion

Wordsworth idea of a new theory of poetry is very good given by him in 'Preface' addition. He gives commitment to all poets who write poetry to be written in simple language. Thus, Wordsworth gives a new meaning or definition of poet and also poetry. In 'Preface' Wordsworth give a new theory of poetry.

XI

Biographia Literaria by Samuel Taylor Coleridge

Scan for the video

Samuel Taylor Coleridge

Q.1. What according to Coleridge is the difference between Fancy and Primary Imagination?

Or

How is primary Imagination different from Secondary Imagination? Fancy and Imagination.

Introduction: The autobiographical work Biographia Literaria by S.T. Coleridge was published in 1817. It was one of the Coleridge's main critical studies.

Samuel Taylor Coleridge (21 October 1772 – 25 July 1834) was an English poet, literary critic, philosopher, and theologian who, with his friend William Wordsworth, was a founder of the Romantic Movement in England.

Coleridge intended Biographia Literaria to be a short preface to a collection of his poems, Sibylline Leaves (1817). However, it quickly expanded into a two-volume autobiography.

In his work he discussed the elements of writing. In one of the most famous passages in Biographia Literaria, Coleridge offers a theory of creativity. Coleridge tries to discover the difference between fancy and imagination. Then he further divided imagination into Primary and Secondary imagination.

· Biographia Literaria is concerned with the form of poetry, the genius of the poet and the relationship to philosophy. Coleridge feels that all of the great writers had their basis in philosophy because philosophy was the sum of all knowledge at this time. All education at that time consisted of a study of philosophy.

· Coleridge examines issues like the use of language in poetry and how it relates to everyday speech. He looks at the relationship between the subject of poetry and its relationship to everyday life.

· Coleridge examines the sources of poetic power which relates to the brilliance of the poet. This involves the use of language, meter, rhyme, and the writing style or the poetic diction.

· **Coleridge builds his Theory on the basic distinction between fancy and imagination.** He first refers to this significance distinction in chapter 4 of Biographia Literaria. During the 17th century , the terms 'imagination' and 'fancy' had almost been used in a synonymous sense.

The 18th century accorded a superior sense first to one term and then to the other, but finally, by the end of the century imagination came to be finely established as the superior term.

It was Wordsworth's reading of a poem in manuscript that aroused Coleridge's interest in the problem of imagination and fancy.

The poem had a deep impact upon him. Pondering over the reasons for this, he concludes that fancy and imagination were two distinct and widely different faculties instead of being same. As illustration , he asserts that "Milton had a highly imaginative, where as Cowley had a very fancy full mind.

· **Coleridge considers fancy to be inferior of the two** . He does not see it as a creative power at all. It only combines what it perceives into pleasing shapes.

In Coleridge's view, Fancy is a kind of memory that arbitrarily brings together images, which continue to their separate and individual properties.

He also uses the term "fancy" as the lowest of all forms of imagination that only has the power to transform already existing ideas and not the creation of new ideas through expression.

Imagination denotes the working of poetic minds upon internal objects or the invisible objects. Imagination process sometimes adds additional properties to an object or sometimes abstracts from some of its properties. Therefore, imagination transforms the object into something new. It modifies and creates new objects.

Imagination is a creative power. It can give shape and forms of beauty by fusing and unifying the different impression it receives from the external world.

The chapter XIII of "Biographia Literaria", deals with the distinction between primary and secondary imagination.

For Coleridge the primary imagination is the elemental power of basic human perception which enable us to identify, to discriminate, to synthesize and then to produce order out of disorder.

The primary imagination then is in every human mind.

The secondary quality is very rare, exclusive active capacity which we call the artistic process. Secondary imagination is a magical synthetic power which makes artistic creation possible. This magical faculty is enjoyed exclusively by artist.

Conclusion:

Biographia Literaria by Samuel Taylor Coleridge is one of the world's most significant treatises on the nature of poetry and the poet. The most important of Coleridge's contributions lies in his theory of the Imagination. He dismisses Fancy as the mere shuffling of sense data and memory by talent. He distinguishes between primary imagination and secondary imagination. The secondary imagination is the creative gift possessed by poetic genius. From the Greek, Coleridge coins the word 'esemplastic' to refer to this imagination which can balance or reconcile the apparent opposites in experience.

XII
Willing Suspension of Disbelief

Scan for the video

Introduction:

Samuel Taylor Coleridge, a leader of the Romantic Movement in English poetry, defined the term "willing suspension of disbelief" in his "Biographia Literaria" (1817) as the reader's suppression of critical analysis and realism for the sake of literary enjoyment. In other words, a reader should not let facts or logic get in the way of a good story, no matter how implausible.

Concept of Willing Suspension of Disbelief.

Suspension of disbelief, sometimes called willing suspension of disbelief, is the avoidance of critical thinking or logic in examining something unreal or impossible in reality, such as a work of speculative fiction, in order to believe it for the sake of enjoyment. Aristotle first explored the idea of the concept in its relation to the principles of theater; the audience ignores the unreality of fiction in order to experience catharsis.

Biographia Literaria contains the first instance of the phrase 'suspension of disbelief'. Writing about his contributions to the Lyrical Ballads, which includes The Rime of the Ancient Mariner, Coleridge says that although his characters were 'supernatural, or at least romantic', he tried to give them a 'human interest and a semblance of disbelief' that would prompt readers to the 'willing suspension of disbelief ... which constitutes poetic faith'.

Coleridge sought to revive the use of fantastic elements in poetry and developed a concept to support how a modern, enlightened audience might continue to enjoy such types of literature. The term resulted from a philosophical experiment, which Coleridge conducted with William Wordsworth within the context of the creation and reading of poetry. It involved an attempt to explain the supernatural persons or characters so that these creatures of imagination constitute some semblance of truth.

XIII

A Defence of Poetry by P.B Shalley

Scan for the video

P.B Shalley

Q.1 What according to Shelley is the contribution of poetry to the fabric of society?

Or

How does Shelley defend poetry in his essay defence of poetry?

Ans.

Introduction:

"A Defence of Poetry" is an essay by the English poet Percy Bysshe Shelley, written in 1821 and first published posthumously in 1840 in Essays, Letters from Abroad. One of the most important prose works of the Romantic era, and a valuable document concerning Shelley's own poetic approach, the essay is deserving of closer analysis and engagement.

Shelley wrote A Defense of poetry in response to an essay written by his friend Thomas Love Peacock i.e The Four Ages of Poetry.

This essay was published in 1840, 18 years after the death of author.

It contains Shelley's famous claim **that "poet are the unacknowledged legislators of the world".**

In **"The Four Ages of Poetry,"** Peacock satirically argues that poetry is no longer needed amid the great technological and scientific advancements of the Industrial Age. He adds that poetry was once useful for awakening the intellect of society, but now humanity has advanced beyond it. Peacock also said the poets of his era were derivative, which showed the downfall of poetry.

Responding to Peacock's critiques in "A Defence of Poetry," Shelley argues that poetry is imperative to society. He does this by first differentiating between reason and imagination, and then he claims that reason serves imagination.

Shelley says that reason is logical thought, whereas imagination is perceiving things, and noticing the similarities between things. It is through reason but also through imagination that we can identify beauty in the world, and from such a perception or realisation are great civilizations made. Poets, then, are the makers of civilization itself, as Shelley argues:

poets, or those who imagine and express this indestructible order, are not only the authors of language and of music, of the dance, and architecture, and statuary, and painting: they are the institutors of laws, and the founders of civil society, and the inventors of the arts of life, and the teachers, who draw into a certain propinquity with the beautiful and the true that partial apprehension of the agencies of the invisible world which is called religion.

The poet throughout history has been both legislator (law-maker) and prophet (religious messenger). And because poets work within the medium of language (unlike the sculptor or painter, who works in the visual medium), they have attained a greater degree of fame than other artists.

Shelley distinguishes between 'measured' and 'unmeasured' language, the former being poetry (which uses metre, i.e., you measure out the syllables per line) and the latter being prose. **Poetry is superior to prose,** even though both use language, because poetry also taps into the possibilities of sounds: 'the language of poets has ever affected a certain uniform and harmonious recurrence of sound, without which it were not poetry, and which is scarcely less indispensable to the communication of its influence, than the words themselves, without reference to that peculiar order.'

Shelley also makes a distinction between storytelling and poetry, arguing, 'A story of particular facts is as a mirror which obscures and distorts that which should be beautiful; poetry is a mirror which makes beautiful that which is distorted.' Poetry thus reflects the world, like a mirror, but does so in a way that renders the distorted image beautiful.

Indeed, poetry can make us see the world in a new light, making it richer and more beautiful:

Poetry lifts the veil from the hidden beauty of the world, and makes familiar objects be as if they were not familiar; it reproduces all that it represents, and the impersonations clothed in its Elysian light stand thenceforward in the minds of those who have once contemplated them, as memorials of that gentle and exalted content which extends itself over all thoughts and actions with which it coexists.

The key to all of this, Shelley reiterates, is imagination.

Shelley devotes the next portion of 'A Defence of Poetry' to a sort of critical history of poetry from the days of ancient Greece up to the present, considering how, throughout the ages, poets have had a moral influence upon the world.

He argues that, following the Fall of Rome and the establishment of Christianity, it was poets who saved the world from ruin and anarchy: 'the world would have fallen into utter anarchy and darkness, but that there were found poets among the authors of the Christian and chivalric systems of manners and religion, who created forms of opinion and action never before conceived; which, copied into the imaginations of men, became as generals to the bewildered armies of their thoughts.'

He sees the medieval poet Dante (1265-1321) as the 'bridge' between the ancient and modern world. Responding to Peacock, Shelley argues that the poet's purpose is utilitarian, since poetry 'lifts the veil from the hidden beauty of the world', and has a moral purpose. Shelley concludes his essay with the rousing and famous words:

Poets are the hierophants of an unapprehended inspiration; the mirrors of the gigantic shadows which futurity casts upon the present; the words which express what they understand not; the trumpets which sing to battle, and feel not what they inspire; the influence which is moved not, but moves. Poets are the unacknowledged legislators of the world.

Conclusion:

Shelley's conclusive remark that "poets are the unacknowledged legislators of the world" suggests his awareness of "the profound ambiguity inherent in linguistic means, which he considers at once as an instrument of intellectual freedom and a vehicle for political and social subjugation".

Block-4 New Criticism

New Criticism was a formalist movement in literary theory that dominated American literary criticism in the middle decades of the 20th century. It emphasized close reading, particularly of poetry, to discover how a work of literature functioned as a self-contained, self-referential aesthetic object. The movement derived its name from John Crowe Ransom's 1941 book The New Criticism.

The work of Cambridge scholar I. A. Richards, especially his Practical Criticism and The Meaning of Meaning, which offered what was claimed to be an empirical scientific approach, were important to the development of New Critical methodology. Also very influential were the critical essays of T. S. Eliot, such as "Tradition and the Individual Talent" and "Hamlet and His Problems", in which Eliot developed his notions of the "theory of impersonality" and "objective correlative" respectively. Eliot's evaluative judgments, such as his condemnation of Milton and Dryden, his liking for the so-called metaphysical poets, and his insistence that poetry must be impersonal, greatly influenced the formation of the New Critical canon.

XIV
Formalism theory

Scan for the video

New Criticism developed as a reaction to the older philological and literary history schools of the US North, which focused on the history and meaning of individual words and their relation to foreign and ancient languages, comparative sources, and the biographical circumstances of the authors, taking this approach under the influence of nineteenth-century German scholarship. The New Critics felt that this approach tended to distract from the text and meaning of a poem and entirely neglect its aesthetic qualities in favor of teaching about external factors. On the other hand, the New Critics disparaged the literary appreciation school, which limited itself to pointing out the "beauties" and morally elevating qualities of the text, as too subjective and emotional. Condemning this as a version of Romanticism, they aimed for a newer, systematic and objective method.

It was felt, especially by creative writers and by literary critics outside the academy, that the special aesthetic experience of poetry and literary language was lost in the welter of extraneous erudition and emotional effusions. Heather Dubrow notes that the prevailing focus of literary scholarship was on "the study of ethical values and philosophical issues through literature, the tracing of literary history, and ... political criticism". Literature was approached via its moral, historical and social background and literary scholarship did not focus on analysis of texts.

New Critics believed the structure and meaning of the text were intimately connected and should not be analyzed separately. In order to bring the focus of literary studies back to analysis of the texts, they aimed to exclude the reader's response, the author's intention, historical and cultural contexts, and moralistic bias from their analysis. These goals were articulated in Ransom's "Criticism, Inc." and Allen Tate's "Miss Emily and the Bibliographer".

Close reading was a staple of French literary studies, but in the United States, aesthetic concerns and the study of modern poets were the province of non-academic essayists and book reviewers rather than serious scholars. The New Criticism changed this. Though their interest in textual study initially met with resistance from older scholars, the methods of the New Critics rapidly predominated in American universities until challenged by feminist literary criticism and structuralism in the 1970s. Other schools of critical theory, including, post-structuralism, and deconstructionist theory, the New Historicism, and Reception studies followed.

Although the New Critics were never a formal group, an important inspiration was the teaching of John Crowe Ransom of Kenyon College, whose students, Allen Tate, Cleanth Brooks, and Robert Penn Warren would go on to develop the aesthetics that came to be known as the New Criticism. Indeed, for Paul Lauter, a Professor of American Studies at Trinity College, New Criticism is a reemergence of the Southern Agrarians.[4] In his essay, "The New Criticism", Cleanth Brooks notes that "The New Critic, like the Snark, is a very elusive beast", meaning that there was no clearly defined "New Critical" manifesto, school, or stance. Nevertheless, a number of writings outline inter-related New Critical ideas.

In 1946, William K. Wimsatt and Monroe Beardsley published a classic and controversial New Critical essay entitled "The Intentional Fallacy", in which they argued strongly against the relevance of an author's intention, or "intended meaning" in the analysis of a literary work. For Wimsatt and Beardsley, the words on the page were all that mattered; importation of meanings from outside the text was considered irrelevant, and potentially distracting.

In another essay, "The Affective Fallacy", which served as a kind of sister essay to "The Intentional Fallacy" Wimsatt and Beardsley also discounted the reader's personal emotional reaction to a literary work as a valid means of analyzing a text. This fallacy would later be repudiated by theorists from the reader-response school of literary theory. One of the leading theorists from this school, Stanley Fish, was himself trained by New Critics. Fish criticizes Wimsatt and Beardsley in his essay "Literature in the Reader" (1970).

The hey-day of the New Criticism in American high schools and colleges was the Cold War decades between 1950 and the mid-seventies. Brooks and Warren's Understanding Poetry and Understanding Fiction both became staples during this era.

Studying a passage of prose or poetry in New Critical style required careful, exacting scrutiny of the passage itself. Formal elements such as rhyme, meter, setting, characterization, and plot were used to identify the theme of the text. In addition to the theme, the New Critics also looked for paradox, ambiguity, irony, and tension to help establish the single best and most unified interpretation of the text.

Although the New Criticism is no longer a dominant theoretical model in American universities, some of its methods (like close reading) are still fundamental tools of literary criticism, underpinning a number of subsequent theoretic approaches to literature including poststructuralism, deconstruction theory, New Testament narrative criticism, and reader-response theory. It has been credited with anticipating the insights of the linguistic turn and for showing significant ideological and historical parallels with logical positivism.

Cleanth Brooks, in his essay "The New Criticism" (1979), argued that the New Criticism was not diametrically opposed to the general principles of reader-response theory and that the two could complement one another. For instance, he stated, "If some of the New Critics have preferred to stress the writing rather than the writer, so have they given less stress to the reader—to the reader's response to the work. Yet no one in his right mind could forget the reader. He is essential for 'realizing' any poem or novel. ... Reader response is certainly worth studying." However, Brooks tempers his praise for the reader-response theory by noting its limitations, pointing out that, "to put meaning and valuation of a literary work at the mercy of any and every individual [reader] would reduce the study of literature to reader psychology and to the history of taste."

Another objection against New Criticism is that it misguidedly tries to turn literary criticism into an objective science, or at least aims at "bringing literary study to a condition rivaling that of science." One example of this is Ransom's essay "Criticism, Inc.", in which he advocated that "criticism must become more scientific, or precise and systematic". René Wellek, however, argued against this by noting that a number of the New Critics outlined their theoretical aesthetics in contrast to the "objectivity" of the sciences.

XV
Practical Criticism by I.A Richard

Scan for the video

Ivor Armstrong Richards

Q.1 Write a note on Practical Criticism.
Ans.
Introduction:

Ivor Armstrong Richards – poet, dramatist, speculative philosopher, psychologist and semanticist, is among the first of the 20th century critics to bring to English criticism a scientific precision and objectivity. He is often referred to as the 'critical consciousness' of the modern age. New Criticism and the whole of modern poetics derive their strength and inspiration from the seminal writings of Richards such as Principles of Literary Criticism, Practical Criticism, Coleridge on Imagination, The Foundation of Aesthetics and The Meaning of Meaning.

Practical criticism is a form of literary analysis which focuses exclusively on the text, ignoring such extraneous factors as authorial intention and historical context. The term originates with an experiment performed on Cambridge literature students by I.A. Richards.

Practical Criticism

Richard's influence rests primarily on his Practical Criticism (1929) which is based on his experiments conducted in Cambridge in which he distributed poems, stripped of all evidence of authorship and period, to his pupils and asked them to comment on them. He analyses factors responsible for misreading of poems. Even a "reputable scholar" is vulnerable to these problems.

1) First is the difficulty of making out the plain sense of poetry. A large proportion of average-to-good readers of poetry simply fail to understand it. They fail to make out its prose sense, it's plain, overt meaning. They misapprehend its feeling, its tone, and its intention.

2) Parallel to the difficulties of interpreting the meaning are the difficulties of sensuous apprehension. Words have a movement and may have a rhythm even when read silently. Many a reader of poetry cannot naturally perceive this.

3) There are difficulties presented by imagery, principally visual imagery, in poetic reading. Images aroused in one mind may not be similar to the ones stirred by the same line of poetry in another, and both may have nothing to do with the images that existed in the poet's mind.

4) Then comes the persuasive influence of mnemonic irrelevancies i.e., the intrusion of private and personal associations.

5) Another is the critical trap called stock responses, based on privately established judgments. These happen when a poem seems to involve views and emotions already fully prepared in the reader's mind.

6) Sentimentality, i.e., excessive emotions

7) Inhibition, i.e., hardness of heart are also perils to understanding poetry.

8) Doctrinal adhesions present another troublesome problem. The views and beliefs about the world contained in poetry could become a fertile source of confusion and erratic judgment.

9) Technical presuppositions too can pose a difficulty. When something has once been done in a certain fashion, we tend to expect similar things to be done in the future in the same fashion, and are disappointed or do not recognize them if they are done differently. This is to judge poetry from outside by technical details. We put means before ends.

10) Finally, general critical preconceptions resulting from theories about its nature and value come between the reader and the poem.

Conclusion:

The objective of Practical Criticism was to encourage students to concentrate on 'the words on the page', rather than rely on preconceived or received beliefs about a text. Richards concludes that the critical reading of poetry is an arduous discipline. "The lesson of all criticism is that we have nothing to rely upon in making our choices but ourselves." The lesson of good poetry, when we have understood it, lies in the degree to which we can order ourselves. Through close analysis of poems and by responding to the emotion and meaning in them the students were to achieve what Richards called an 'organized response.' From this stems Richard's 'psychologism' which is concerned not with the poem per se but with the responses to it.

XVI
Principle of Literary Criticism by I.A Richard

Scan for the video

Introduction:

Ivor Armstrong Richards – poet, dramatist, speculative philosopher, psychologist and semanticist, is among the first of the 20th century critics to bring to English criticism a scientific precision and objectivity. He is often referred to as the 'critical consciousness' of the modern age. New Criticism and the whole of modern poetics derive their strength and inspiration from the seminal writings of Richards such as Principles of Literary Criticism, Practical Criticism, Coleridge on Imagination, The Foundation of Aesthetics and The Meaning of Meaning.

In Principles of Literary Criticism, I.A.Richards set out to establish a theoretical framework for criticism which would free it from subjectivity and emotionalism. He some isolated observations which could make profitable starting points for reflection. But they provide no answer to the central question of criticism: "What is the value of the arts, and what is their place in the system of human endeavors?" Richards proposes a psychological theory of art; art is valuable because it helps to order our impulses.

• Principles of literary criticism is one of the first books of the literary Formalism- a study of text without taking into account any outside influence. Formalism rejects notion of culture or societal influence, authorship and content and instead focus on modes, genre, discourse and forms motifs grammar etc.

• In the opening chapter of Principles of Literary Criticism, titled "The Chaos of Critical Theories", Richards points out that the literature of criticism is a rather significant field of study, which dates back to the contribution of the great scholar Aristotle, who is probably the first intellectual to have followed the practice in his age. The modern student, who surveys the field of criticism, would probably be intrigued about the contribution of criticism, its strengths and its incorrect assessments. Criticism is also apprehensive about the nature of experiences and the actual process of using experiences, which are associated with the activities like observing a picture, playing music or reading a book.

• In the second chapter, "The Phantom Aesthetic State", he dismisses the concept of a special aesthetic state. Modern aesthetics, starting with Kant, rests on the assumption that there is a special kind of pleasure which is disinterested, universal, unintellectual and not to be confused with the pleasures of sense or ordinary emotions. They believed that art experience was a special kind of experience, in a class of its own, not to be compared with the experiences of ordinary life.

• Richards states that several chapters are lengthy discourses on value and many of them deal with general psychology. The use of psychology was unavoidable because of its relevance in explaining several aspects of the value of art. He also expresses the view that the chapters employ illustrations to be applied to the statements made so that the reader

could actively participate in judging the appropriateness of the arguments presented before them.

· I.A Richard brought a rigorous scientific approach to building this system. He thought that literature is all about the experience of the reader and the way that the reader reacts to the text is explained through psychology.

· He says, science is our mechanism of uncovering the world for our use of it. Literature is our mechanism for finding our place in the world. We need to be human being.

Conclusion:

Principles of Literary Criticism directly points out to the activity of deriving value from the arts, especially the art of poetry. In many ways, the basis of all Richards' statements on criticism, this argument sets into action, the fundamental critical and artistic theories in search of value of art. He begins this complex study by indicating several impediments, which often preclude valid criticism. The first is, "experimental aesthetics" in the arts, where futile attempts are made with human tastes and actions to suit laboratory examination. Second, criticism tends to concentrate on secondary aspects of the arts and thereby ignores the subject of value. Third, the language of criticism causes misunderstanding because of its vague, often deceiving vocabulary. A suitable instance would be the critics who speak of objects of art as if the objects themselves possess qualities, whereas what they should say is that the objects evoke effects in us.

XVII

Tradition and Individual Talent by T.S.Eliot

Scan for the video

Thomas Stearns Eliot

Introduction:

"Tradition and the Individual Talent" (1919) is an essay written by poet and literary critic T. S. Eliot. The essay was first published in The Egoist (1919) and later in Eliot's first book of criticism, "The Sacred Wood" (1920). The essay is also available in Eliot's "Selected Prose" and "Selected Essays".

While Eliot is most often known for his poetry, he also contributed to the field of literary criticism. In this dual role, he acted as a cultural critic, comparable to Sir Philip Sidney and Samuel Taylor Coleridge. "Tradition and the Individual Talent" is one of the better-known works that Eliot produced in his critic capacity. It formulates Eliot's influential conception of the relationship between the poet and preceding literary traditions.

Content of the essay: This essay is divided into three parts: first the concept of "Tradition," then the Theory of Impersonal Poetry, and finally the conclusion. The essay Tradition and the Individual Talent is an attack on certain critical views in Romanticism particularly up on the idea that a poem is primarily an expression of the personality of the poet.

In part 1, Eliot articulates his concept of literary tradition. He argues that often what marks great poetry is the degree to which it is in conversation with the poetry of the past.

In his view, to be "traditional" is not to lack originality, but rather to possess an awareness of the "whole of the literature of Europe."

Innovation and creativity are important, but truly accomplished poets must understand how their works relate to both the present and the past.

Essentially, Eliot claims that poetry does not exist in a vacuum and that the meaning of a poem is never defined solely by its contents. Instead, all art is in conversation with itself, with each new generation's contributions expanding and altering the ways in which the literary canon as a whole is understood. Thus, tradition and individual talent go together.

Tradition is the gift of the historic sense. A writer with this sense of tradition is fully conscious of his own generation, of his place in the present, but he is also acutely conscious of his relationship with the writers of the past.

In part 2, Eliot expands on his belief that the creation of poetry is an act of depersonalization. He argues that the mature poet writes not because he has "more to say" but because his technique has made it possible for him to more finely articulate emotion.

He explains this using an analogy from chemistry: platinum, in the presence of oxygen and sulfur dioxide, acts as a catalyst to create sulfurous acid, but remains itself unchanged. The poet is akin to the platinum in this reaction: through the creation of art, new work is brought into being, but the poet is unchanged.

Building on his concept of the poet as an impersonal medium, Eliot asserts that great art is not an expression of the poet's personal emotions but rather an act of aesthetic distillation. Instead of depicting novel or uniquely potent emotions, the poet must instead collect ordinary "feelings, phrases, images" and synthesize them into a "new compound." This new compound does not achieve greatness from the intensity of its components but rather from the rigors of the "artistic process" that the poet subjects them to. The end result should transcend the more personal experiences of emotion and feeling. Thus the poem arrives at a broader aesthetic sensibility that is self-contained yet converses with the works of the past, present, and future.

Conclusion:

Part 3 offers a short conclusion and advocates for shifting critical focus away from poets and onto the poems themselves. Eliot reiterates his argument that "the emotion of art is impersonal." In his view, the work of poets is not to convey their own "sincere emotion," but rather to act as a medium through which the collective thoughts, feelings, and emotions of the living "mind of Europe" are conveyed.

XVIII

Intentional Fallacy and Affective Fallacy

Scan for the video

Introduction:

William Kurtz Wimsatt was an American professor of English, literary theorist and critic. Wimsatt is often associated with the concepts of the intentional fallacy and affective fallacy, which he developed with Monroe Beardsley in order to discuss the importance of an author's intentions for creation of a work of art and error of judging or evaluating a text on the basis of its emotional effects on a reader.

Intentional fallacy:

It is a kind of mistake of deriving meaning of the text in terms of author's intention, feeling, emotion, attitude, biography and situation. It is the error of interpreting a literary work by reference to evidence according to the intention of the author.

Intentional fallacy means the confusion between the poem and its origin. It is the fallacy because an author is not the part of the text; instead, text is public but not private.

If a critic interprets text in terms of author's biography, this interpretation is called subjective interpretation or criticism. But for Wimsatt and Beardsley criticism should be objective and textual, critic should not go beyond the text.

Author can't control the text as soon as he writes, it becomes public. The critic should not interpret the allusion in terms of author's intention. They claim that author's intended meaning is irrelevant to the literary critic. The meaning, structure, value of text is inherent with in the work of art itself; it is an object with certain autonomy.

Affective Fallacy:

Affective fallacy means the confusion between the poem and its result. It is a way of deriving meaning of the text interims of effect of product up on the reader.

Affective fallacy is the error of evaluating a text by its effect. As a result of this fallacy, criticism ends in impressionism and relativism and objective criticism becomes almost impossible. Theories of catharsis, therapy, didacticism etc., fall under the affective fallacy because they judge the poem in terms of its effect on the reader.

Wimsatt and Breadsley view that text constitutes language. The meaning of test is public, not personal. The effect of the text varies from person to person and from reading to reading. Thus, if the critic depends on the meaning produced by a single reader it will be a kind of mistake.

As a text is an autonomous entity, the best way of deriving meaning is to analyze linguistics elements such as syntax, semantics etc., since the work of art has its own anthological status, and it should not be judged through the parameter outside the text.

Wimsatt and Brendsley criticize the tradition of expressive criticism as intentional fallacy and pragmatic criticism as affective fallacy. They believe that a work of literature or text has ontology of its own. It is not only an autonomous object but also complete in itself.

So it has no need to take support of writer's intention and reader's affective response to assert its being. It can have its meaning with in itself, by its own structure. So its own being should be the subject of critical study.

Conclusion:

In the end, Wimsatt and Beardsley ask for more of a formalist mode of criticism that looks to evaluate the value of a work of art through an analysis of artistic qualities. Though the intention of the author and the reader's response is most of the time mentioned in New Critical interpretation of a literary text, neither one is the center of investigation. There is only one way by which we can find out whether the author's intention or a readers' interpretation of a literary text truly put forward the meaning of a text and that is by scrupulously studying or "close reading" of all the evidence provided by the text itself: symbols, metaphors, rhyme, meter and so forth.

XIX

The language of paradox
by Cleanth Brooks

Scan for the video

Cleanth Brooks

Q.1 The 'truth which the poet utters' according to Cleanth Brooks, 'can be approached only in terms of paradox'. Do you agree?

Introduction:

'The Language of Paradox' is an essay by Cleanth Brooks. Cleanth Brooks (1906—1994), an American teacher and critic whose work was important in establishing New Criticism.

His best-know works, The Well-Wrought Urn: Studies in the Structure of Poetry and Modern Poetry and the Tradition. He argued for the centrality of ambiguity and paradox a way of understanding poetry.

With his writings, Brooks helped to formulate formalist criticism, emphasizing "the interior life of a poem" and codifying the principles of close reading.

Summary:

'The Language of Paradox', the first chapter of Cleanth Brooks' Well-wrought Urn, begins with the famous statement: '...the language of poetry is the language of paradox'. Paradox is the language of 'sophistry, hard, bright' and 'witty' and not the language of poetry. 'Our prejudices force us to regard paradox as intellectual rather than emotional, clever rather than profound, rational rather than divinely irrational'. The scientist may need freedom from paradox, but for the poet, truth can be 'approached', only through paradox.

Analysis:

• Cleanth Brooks advocate the centrality of paradox as a way of understanding and interpreting poetry.

• In "The Language of Paradox", Brooks establishes the crucial role of paradox by demonstrating that paradox is the language appropriate and inevitable to poetry, it is not merely a literary device so he states that language of poetry is the language of paradox.

• In this essay he has shown how the poet conveys his thought and ideas by using a literary device like paradox without employing a direct statement in poetry.

• Brooks emphasizes how the language of poetry is different from that of the sciences, claiming that he is interested in our seeing that the paradoxes spring from the very nature of the poet's language.

• Brooks stresses that poetic language is inherently different from scientific language because the poet constructs his language as he goes and defines his own rules. The poet, then has control over language, and must take an active role in the shaping of what literature means.

• He has exhibited that the connotative meaning achieved by the poet is by using a paradox. The reader know that paradox is not a literary device for conveying the inner and warm thoughts and emotion; It is not a language of soul. Paradox is often used in a language of refinement and sophistry. It is quite unnatural. Hence no one would agree with the view that language of poetry is the language of paradox.

• As a literary device, paradox can be deemed as a intellectual rather than emotional aspect. But Brooks asserts that paradox is the most appropriate and ideal device to poetry in order to convey thoughts as well as emotion. He thinks that the language employed in science is refined and clear and it is free from paradoxical statements.

•Brooks quotes paradoxes from Wordsworth, a poet who insisted on simplicity and was suspicious of sophistication. He quotes the sonnet 'It is a Beauteous Evening' as an example. The sonnet highlights a paradoxical situation.

The poet is filled with divine thoughts, unlike the girl. But her nature is not less divine. She worships more deeply as her mind is filled with an unconscious sympathy (unconscious worship) for all of Nature. As Coleridge wrote: He prayed best, who loveth best/ All things both great and small.

• Then Brooks takes up another sonnet: "Composed upon Westminster Bridge." Many readers cannot account for the poem's greatness. There is very little 'nobility' in the sentiments. The images are neither graphic nor realistic. The sonnet contains 'some very flat writing' and 'well-worn comparisons. Despite these drawbacks, the poem becomes great because of 'the paradoxical situation' from which it is born.

It is a paradox that 'grimy, feverish' London can "wear the beauty of the morning". Mount Snowden or Mont Blanc can 'wear beauty by natural right', but not London. 'Man-made London is a part of nature too, is lighted by the Sun of nature, and lighted to as beautiful effect'. The 'stale metaphor' ('sleeping houses') in the last two lines is revitalized because the poet sees the city as organic, and not mechanical. He thought the houses dead but now realizes that they were only asleep.

• Brooks end his essay with a reading of John Donne's poem "The Canonization", which uses a paradox as its underlying metaphor. Using a charged religious term to describe the speaker's physical love as saintly.

Donne effectively argues that in rejecting the material world and withdrawing to a world of each other, the two lovers are appropriate candidates for canonization.

This seems to parody both love and religion, but in fact it combines them, pairing unlikely circumstances and demonstrating their resulting complex meaning.

Conclusion:

Brooks believes that the very structure of poetry is paradox, and ignores the other subtleties of imagination and power that poets bring to their poems.

Also, by defining poetry as uniquely having a structure of paradox, Brooks ignores the power of paradox in everyday conversation and discourse, including scientific discourse, which Brooks claimed was opposed to poetry.

XX

Criticism Inc. by John Crowe Ransom

Scan for the video

John Crowe Ransom

Introduction

John Crowe Ransom (1888-1974) was an American Literary critic. He was the founder of New Criticism. New Criticism was a formalist movement that emphasized the 'closed reading' of the text. It argues that the words on the page are the most important elements within the analysis.

New Criticism looked at the idea of a text in an aesthetic form. In other words, there was a shift within the analysis from socio-cultural aspects around a text to the internals within a text. So a text's internal world becomes the site of focus within New Criticism. He was a member of Fugitives. The fugitive was a group of social scientists that was rooted in the preservation of classical and traditional values and styles.

John Crowe Ransom's New Criticism, 1941, proposes the following ideas – Text becomes the focus of closed-reading. The analysis of a text has to be scientific and precise. Personal, historical, moral and biographical details around a text are all rejected in the field of New Criticism.

The idea was to take the focus of the reader closer to things inside a text rather than things outside of a text. So a lot of information that exists outside a text is rejected through New Criticism. The idea is similar to I.A. Richard's "closed-reading" approach.

Closed Reading within New Criticism advocated the sanctity of the act of reading written words on the page. For instance – any extract from a book can be picked up in isolation from the book or author, and an analysis is carried out on the particular extract without bleeding into the rest of the context.

New Criticism focused on the purity of a text and the purity of the act of reading, analyzing without bothering about historical or political perspectives around the text. It serves an aesthetic purpose where a text becomes significant for the sake of itself. New Criticism takes the idea of text as an isolated cerebral process away from politics, morality, history, etc.

Q.1 What does Ransom mean when he advocates "Criticism Inc"?

Or

What according to John Crowe Ransom is the role of the literary critic in the modern world? Explain.

John Crowe Ransom, in his seminal 1937 essay, ***"Criticism, Inc."*** Ransom laid out his ideal form of literary criticism stating that, "criticism must become more scientific, or precise and systematic." To this end, he argued that personal responses to literature, historical scholarship, linguistic scholarship, and what he termed "moral studies" should not influence literary criticism. He also argued that literary critics should regard a poem as an aesthetic object. Many of the ideas he explained in this essay would become very important in the development of The New Criticism.

"Criticism Inc." which was first published in the Virginia Quarterly Review in 1937, makes a strong plea for the development of literary criticism as a distinct discipline in universities.

. It expresses the New Critics' concept of what criticism should be—a collaborative effort in the elucidation and evaluation of literary texts, including contemporary works.

He attacks other rival approaches: historical scholarship, impressionistic, emotional appreciation, and the various kinds of criticism which focus on the abstracted content of a work of literature instead 'of the work itself.

The essay begins by reviewing the current state of criticism: "critics nearly always have been amateurs", they feel that no special training is needed to be a literary critic.

According to Ransom, the critic needs the kind of competence that **three different people possess:theartist, the philosopher, and the university teacher of English.**But each profession has its drawbacks. The artist's evaluation is intuitive, he cannot explain it to others; however, practitioners often make the best critics as T.S. Eliot also believed in his later writings, because they have a good command of the language. The philosopher knows the function of the fine arts, but his theory is too general-he cannot appreciate the technical effects. He has no intimate knowledge of a particular works of art, and his generalizations are drawn not from observation and study, but from other generalizations. The professors should take charge of critical activity, but they are not critical enough. They are learned men who are ready to spend a lifetime in compiling the data of literature, but they avoid making literary judgement. Ransom insists that it is the duty of the university professors to set up proper standards of criticism. Criticism should be developed by the systematic effort of learned persons, and the proper place for this is the university.

Though Ransom suggests that criticism should be made scientific, he does not mean that it can ever be an exact science. What he means is that it should be systematic, and professionals should take charge of it. Hence the title of the essay: he wants criticism to be established as a profession, "what we need is 'Criticism Inc.'", he says. In India, when serious entrepreneurs establish a company, they engage professionals to run it, and it is called "Ltd." (short for "Limited"). In America, the preferred term is "Inc.", an abbreviation for "Incorporated", which is added to the name of a company. For- example, you have "The New India Assurance Company Ltd." or "Sun Microsystems Inc."

He gives due credit to R.S.Crane, Professor at the University of Chicago, (who led a group called the "Chicago Critics"); he was the first of the professors to advocate the study of criticism as an academic discipline. In his influential article, "History versus

Criticism in the University Study of Literature" (first published in 1935):' Crane said that the emphasis must be shifted to the critical from the historical in literary studies.

Ransom attacks other contemporary schools. The Humanists (Irving Babbitt, W.C. Brownell and Paul Elmer More, among others) had adopted an approach different from historical scholarship; but they failed to provide objective criticism, they were engaged in advocating a certain moral system. For Ransom, "Criticism is the attempt to define and enjoy the aesthetic or characteristic values of literature", but the preoccupations of Irving Babbitt are ethical, not literary. Another diversion from objective evaluation of literature is provided by the Leftists or Proletarians; these Marxist critics want literature to "serve the cause of loving-comradeship", they are not interested in literary values, the last a judgement only vulgar Marxists and not genuine Marxist critics would endorse.

He advocates an autonomous school of English studies; it should not be a branch of the department of history, or of the department of ethics. It is wrong to think that just anybody, without specific training, can be a critic. He gives examples from other fields: in economics, chemistry, sociology, theology or architecture, criticism of the performance is in the hands of men who have had formal training in its theory and technique. Literary criticism, too, should be a specialized discipline.

In the third section of the essay, he considers what the duties of a critic should be. Departments of English have to communicate the understanding of literature, but professors should not content themselves with just reading the text well, hoping that the students will somehow learn to appreciate it. A teacher who stops with exposing students to the text is compared to the curator of a museum, who shows works of art to an audience. He is not an instructor. Historical scholarship is important; but it is not the end, it is only instrumental. Like linguistic study, historical study is a necessary aid, it is indispensable for a true understanding of the text. "We can never have too much of it" declares Ransom, "if the critical intelligence functions, and has the authority to direct it."

In Section IV, Ransom sets out to define criticism. He proceeds by explaining "what criticism is not". He begins by excluding book reviews, and (following Crane,) works of historical scholarship and Neo-Humanism. He presents a list of six items which he considers to be not literary criticism.

1. Personal registration. Describing the effect of the work of art on the reader cannot be considered literary criticism. Criticism should be concerned with describing "the nature of the object rather than its effects on the subject". This is a point developed fully by Wimsatt and Beardsley in "The Affective Fallacy". To say that the reader is moved to tears is not an analysis of the text.

Ransom says' that even Aristotle succumbed to this fallacy in his theory of "catharsis", though other parts of the Poetics present fine objective criticism of tragedy. Judging by effects denies the autonomy of the work. A text is something which exists for its own sake. Ransom warns us against using words loosely. We should not ascribe qualities to the object which actually apply to the subjective effect: moving, exciting, entertaining, pitiful etc.

2. Synopsis and paraphrase. It may be necessary to discuss the content of a work when analysing it, but we must always keep in mind that the story or the plot is an abstract, the true content of a work cannot be isolated from

it. Discussing the synopsis of a novel or the prose paraphrase of a poem does not amount to literary criticism.

3. Historical studies. Understanding the general literary background, the author's biography, autobiographical evidence, bibliographical items, and knowledge of the literary originals can all be useful aids to literary criticism, but they do not constitute it.

4. Linguistic studies. Studies concerned with meaning of words and idioms ensure that criticism is based on proper understanding of the text. But linguistic studies alone cannot produce a critic.

5. Moral studies. Individual readers will apply their own moral standards; it may be the Christian ethic, it may be Aristotelian, or Marxist. But the moral content should not be taken as the whole content of the work. Criticism is concerned with the whole content.

6. Any other special studies. Various departments can find relevant material in literature: works can be written from the point of view of sociology, geography, law etc. Discussions of Milton's geography, or Shakespeare's understanding of the law, do not constitute literary criticism. It can be considered literary criticism only when the critic discusses the creative writer's literary assimilation of material pertaining to other disciplines, he can analyse how Milton's or Shakespeare's knowledge of geography or law has become part of his poetry.

In Section V of his essay, Ransom discusses the critical act. He believes that book reviewing cannot be an act of purely literary criticism, because the reviewer has the responsibility of presentation and interpretation as well as criticism. Criticism is an important part of book reviewing, but it involves other things as well, such as telling the reader about the book itself (presentation) and discussing the main themes of the Studies in technique are an important mode of literary criticism. Thus, a critic of poetry would discuss the devices such as metre, inversion, tropes. inventions etc. which differentiate it from ordinary prose. The good critic is not content with just listing the separate devices, he discusses their function. The critic should regard the poem as a metaphysical manoeuvre - Ransom has written elsewhere about his concept of poetry, and we shall read excerpts from his essay on poetry in the next section. The poet presents a total poetic or individual object which tends to be universalized. The critic has to identify the logical object or universal, and the dense technical structure in which it is enmeshed. According to Ransom, there are two aspects to a poem: "the prose core", the universalized object, and the "differentia, residue or tissue which keeps the object poetical or entire." In a later essay, "Criticism as Pure Speculation", he uses the terms' "structure" and "texture" for the same concepts. He feels that this two-fold construction is true of other forms of literature, such as fiction, as also the non-literary arts (like painting, sculpture, music etc.).

Block-5 Marxist view of Literature

XXI
MARXISM AND LITERATURE

Scan for the video

Questions:

1. Discuss the Marxist interpretation of Ideology.

2. Explain how Marxist critics explore the link between ideology and literature.

Ans.

Introduction: Marxism is a political and social movement as well as a critique of capitalism. It presents an analysis of society, its problems and a solution. Its works were written by German philosophers Karl Marx and Friedrich Engels.

Let us understand how do Marx and Engels interpret literature. Marx's major contribution was to the development of its ideas. Engels, on the other hand, contributed ideas and popularized Marxism. Marx and Engels announced a system in Communist Manifesto as Communism based on their ideas. They opposed the domination of one class over another and imagined a classless society.

Marxism analyzes society in terms of class struggle between the oppressed and the oppressor, "The history of all hitherto existing society is the history of class struggles." Marx's Communist Manifesto explains the historical background that led to the development of modern capitalist society wherein the bourgeois (ruling class) exploits the proletariat (working class).

Marx gives the solution to social problems as a classless society whose development is theoreticallybased on the development of each individual. Marxism aims at achieving this goal through the revolutionary process, through the annihilation of the capitalist system.

Marxist literary criticism holds the view that a writer's work is shaped by social institutions and prevailing discourse of his time. It does not regard writers as autonomous individuals. Marxist approach interprets a work of art by putting it into its historical context and analyses conflicts of historical forces and social classes.

The Marxist approach is based on 'dialectical materialism'. The term was coined by German Marxist Joseph Dietzgen in 1887. This concept focuses on the material conditions of society. It emphasizes matter as the fundamental basis of nature. It, thus emphasizes that consciousness is determined by social existence.

Marx viewed that material conditions have contradictions. These contradictions are what Marxism resolves. The concept is inspired by Hegelian dialectics. Marx's dialectics differs from Hegel's in a way that Marx's focus is on material while Hegel sees contradictions in ideas. Hegel holds the view that consciousness determines social existence.

Literature and Ideology

The question of ideology is central in Marxism. Marxist use of the term ideology is different from the use of the term by common people. In ordinary sense, ideology refers to a set of beliefs that people consciously hold – beliefs of which they are aware and which they can articulate. For instance, one can speak of the ideology of the free market, referring to a series of arguments that demands free enterprise against state intervention. In contrast, Marxist notion of ideology is not a set of beliefs or assumptions that we are aware of, but it is that makes us experience our life in a certain way and makes us believe that that way of seeing ourselves and the world is natural. Hans Bertens explains the Marxist notion of ideology:

In Marxist usage, ideology is what causes us to misrepresent the world to ourselves. As for Marxism the basis of any society is its economic organization, which then gives rise to certain social relations – for instance, the class relations between capitalists and workers in nineteenth century Capitalist economies.

Marxist critics argue that if we succumb to ideology, we live in an illusory world in what in Marxism has often been described as a state of 'false consciousness'.

Marxist critics hold the view that dominant ideology hides authentic realities from masses. Louis Althusser presents the thesis that ideology represents the imaginary relationship of individuals to their real conditions of existence. This implies that ideology distorts one's view of his/her real conditions of existence. Althusser also links ideology with its social sources. For Althusser, ideology works through so called ideological State apparatuses, which are all subject to the ruling ideology. Althusser's notion of ideological state apparatuses include organized religion, the law, the political system, the educational system – in short; all the institutions through which human beings are socialized. Ideology, then, has a material existence in the sense that it is embodied in all sorts of material practices. *Althusser mentions some of the practices that are part ofthe material existence of an ideological apparatus, be it only a small part of that apparatus a small mass in a small church, a funeral, a minor match at a sports club, a school day, a political party meeting, etc.*

Althusser implies that ideology is waiting for human beings and that practically everything they do and everything they engage in is pervaded by ideology. He explains:

Ideas have disappeared as such (insofar as they are endowed with an ideal or spiritual existence), to the precise extent that it has emerged that their existence is inscribed in the actions of practices governed by rituals defined in the last instance by an ideological apparatus. It therefore appears that the

subject acts insofar as he is acted by the following system...ideology existing in a material ideological apparatus, prescribing material practices governed by a material ritual, which practices exist in the material actions of a subject acting in all consciousness according to his belief.

Althusser led the way for explorations of the way ideology works in literature. Colin McCabe and other British Marxist critics showed how, for instance, the objective realism of the midnineteenth-century English novel is not so objective at all. They argued that Charlotte Bronte's Jane Eyre (1847) and George Eliot's Middlemarch (1872), which present their characters as essentially free, even if not all of them make use of that freedom, 'hail' us just like ideology hails us. Such novels invite their readers to become part of a world that is essentially free and to make autonomous decisions. Hans Bertens explains the ideological apparatus in such novels:

In doing so they create a specific subject position for their readers and give them the illusion that they, too, are free. Just like ideology, such novels give their readers the idea that they are complete: they make them believe that they are free agents and, in that way, make them complicit in their own delusion.

Marxism and Literature

Basic Marxist perspective on literature is that it is a cultural superstructure which is determined by the socio-economic base. Marx himself was of the view that the developments in art and literature did not necessarily immediately reflect changes in the economic pattern and the relations between classes. The so-called 'vulgar Marxists' of the pre-war period looked at the direct cause effect relationship between the socio-economic base and literature and held that the writer is directly conditioned by his/her social class. They were also concerned about writers' link with ideology. Further, they held the view that the social reality of the writer will always be a part of the text.

Marxist critics also address the question if literary texts can be considered as social evidence. They would ask the question – can Charles Dickens' Great Expectations and George Eliot's Middlemarch be considered as true pictures of Victorian England or ideologically distorted reflections? Georg Lukacs, for instance, considers panoramic novels of Honore de Balzac and Leo Tolstoy to be more socially relevant than the fragmentary avant-garde products. Lukacs argues that a socially committed writer would try to merge individual life stories with larger movements of history. In his essay, "Ideology of Modernism", he observes:

Achilles and Werther, Oedipus and Tom Jones, Antigone and Anna Karenina: their individual existence...cannot be distinguished from their social and historical environment. Their human significance, their specific individuality cannot be separated from their context in which they are created.

The British and American Marxist critics of the 1970 and 1980s were influenced by Althusser and his view that texts do not so easily allow us a view of an undistorted reality.

French critic, Pierre Macherey's views on literature match that of Althusser. For Macherey, literary works are pervaded by ideology. He says, in his work, A Theory of Literary Production, that in order to get beyond a text's ideological dimension, readers will have to begin with the cracks in its façade. He argues that in order to expose a text's ideology, interpretation must paradoxically focus on what the text does not say, on what the text represses rather than expresses.

Marxist critics of the United Kingdom like Terry Eagleton and Terrence Hawkes analyze canonical texts in a way to make the texts turn against themselves. This practice anticipates poststructuralist approach.

Conclusion: In general, one can say that the Marxist critic's interest in ideology is the extension of his/her interest in the link between the ideology of the literary work and the real world. Such a critic explores the politics of the text – its ideological dimension. Marxist Criticism, thus, addresses at once the politics of a text and the politics of the world outside it.

XXII
MARXISM AND LITERARY CRITICISM
by Terry Eagleton

Scan for the video

Questions:

1. Explain Terry Eagleton's view on Literature and Ideology.
2. Discuss Terry Eagleton's opinion on writer's commitment to society as revealed in Marxism and Literary Criticism.

3. Explain how Eagleton makes a Marxist evaluation of the link between form and content in literature.

Ans.

Introduction:

Terry Eagleton is a British literary theorist widely regarded as Britain's most influential living literary critic. He obtained both his M.A. and Ph.D. from Trinity College, Cambridge and then became a fellow of Jesus College, Cambridge. He began his academic life as a Victorianist and is still interested in the history and literature of the 19th century. His specialties are literary and cultural theories. He is also becoming rather more broadly involved in comparative literature. His books of literary criticism include Literary Theory: An Introduction (1983), Marxism and Literary Criticism (1976), After Theory (2003), The Ideology of Aesthetic (1990) and The Illusions of Post Modernism (1996).

Marxism and Literary Criticism: An Overview

Chapter 1: Literature and History

Marxist Criticism analyses literature in terms of the historical conditions, which produce it. It is a part of a larger body of theoretical analysis, which aims to understand ideologies and plays a significant role in the transformation of human societies.

Eagleton explains that Marxist Criticism is not merely a 'sociology of literature' concerned with how literary works are produced, distributed and exchanged in a particular society but aims to explain them more fully by paying attention to their forms, styles and meanings, which are considered as products of a particular history. Though there were many thinkers before Marx, who tried to account the literary works in terms of the history, which produced them, the originality of Marxist Criticism lies in its revolutionary understanding of history itself.

The seeds of this revolutionary understanding are indisputably found in Marx and Engels' The German Ideology (1848) and in the preface to A Contribution to the Critique of Political Economy (1859) in which Marx discusses the relationship between society and basic economic reality. Marx argues that the social relations between men are bound with a manner in which they produced their material life. The simplest Marxist model of society sees it as constituted by a 'base' comprising of the material means of production, distribution and exchange and a 'superstructure', which is the cultural world of ideas, art, religion, law and so on. The essential Marxist view is that the latter things are determined by the nature of the economic base. Terry Eagleton is of the view that art is part of the superstructure of society and society's ideology. So, to understand literature means understanding the total social process of which it is part. He maintains that to comprehend literary works, we have to first understand the complex, indirect relations between those works and the ideological worlds they inhabit – relations which emerge not just in themes, history but also in style, rhythm, image, quality and form. Eagleton elucidates this by explaining the Placido Gulf scene in Courad's Nortromo. He argues that the pessimistic vision represented by the scene cannot be simply analyzed in terms of psychological factors but on the basis of the ideological pessimism rampant due to the history of imperialistic capitalism throughout Courad's time.

In considering the relationship between 'base' and 'superstructure', Eagleton quotes Engels' letter to Joseph Bloch to state the fact that literature, being a part of the superstructure is not merely a passive reflection of the economic base but it continuously and consistently reacts back upon and influence the economic base. As Eagleton aptly says: "The materialist theory of history denies that art can in itself change the course of history; but it insists that art can be an active element in such change . Like Engels, Marx too selects art to consider the complexity and indirectness of the base – superstructure relationship. Marx in his introduction to the Grumdisse states:

"In the case of the arts, it is well known that certain periods of their flowering are out of all proportion to the general development of society, hence also to the material foundation, the skeletal structure as it were, of its organization" .

Marx is of the view that there is an unequal relationship between the development of material production and artistic production. He brings the instance of the Greeks as clear evidence to prove that major art is produced in an economically undeveloped state of society. Marx explains this asymmetrical relationship by stating that each element in society's superstructure has its own pace of development, its own internal evolution, which cannot be relegated to mere expression of class struggle or the state of the economy. This discrepancy is aptly explained by Eagleton by taking the example of T.S. Eliot's The Waste Land. Eagleton says that The Waste Land can be explicated as a poem, which is determined by ideological, political and economic factors (spiritual emptiness, First World War and imperialist Capitalism). But he contends that a complete understanding of The Waste

Land would need to take into account the author's class position (Eliot's ambiguous relationship with English society), ideological forms and their relation to literary forms, spirituality (part Christian part Buddhist), philosophy (Fraser's anthropology), techniques of literary production (experimental, montage, juxtaposition, music-symphony) and aesthetic theory, which are directly relevant to the base / superstructure model. According to Terry Eagleton, what Marxist Criticism looks for is the unique blend of these elements, which we know as The Waste Land. The question of ideology is central in understanding Marxism. In ordinary sense, ideology refers to a set of ideas that people consciously hold and believe in. But, in contrast, Marxist notion of ideology is not a set of beliefs / doctrines but it stands for the way we experience our lives in class-based society. It also signifies the values, ideas and images, which bind us to our social functions and prevent us from true knowledge of society as a whole. It makes us believe that the way of seeing ourselves and our world is natural. Marxists argue that if we surrender to ideology, we are living in an illusory world and this has often been described as 'false consciousness' in Marxism. So, Eagleton argues that if literature is considered as ideology in a certain artistic form, then it would just be expressions of the ideologies of their time, a document of false consciousness. On the other hand, literature also challenges the ideology; it confronts and transcends the ideological limits of its time, providing us insight into the realities, which ideology actually hides from our view. Eagleton provides Althusser's subtle account of the relationship between literature and ideology to further his argument. Althusser explains the relationship by bringing in the difference between science and art. He argues that science gives us conceptual knowledge of a situation and art gives us the experience of that situation, which is equivalent to ideology. But, by doing this, art allows us to see the nature of that ideology and thereby the scientific understanding of the ideology. Althusser's colleague, Pierre Machery goes a step further to explain the relationship between ideology and literature. He claims that illusion (ideology) is the corpus on which the writer begins his work but he transforms it into something different. Literature gives ideology a shape and structure and is able to distance itself from it, thus, revealing to us the limits of that ideology. Thus, Machery claims that literature contributes to our escape from the ideological illusion.

Chapter II – Form and Content

Marxist Criticism has always been in opposition to all kinds of literary Formalism, which it believes, rob literature of historical significance and reduce it to an aesthetic diversion. Marx himself believed that literature should bring about a unity of form and content. Marx makes a comment on formalist writing in Rheinische Zeitung: "Form is of no value unless it is the form of its content" (p20). Marxist Criticism sees form and content as dialectically related but affirms the dominance of content in determining the form. For instance, Hegel states:

"Content is nothing but the transformation of form into content, and form is nothing but the transformation of content into form".

Fredric Jameson too has remarked in his Marxism and Form (1971) "Form itself is but the working out of content in the realm of the superstructure." Eagleton suggests that a significant development in literary form results from significant changes in ideology. The changes embody new ways of perceiving social reality and new relations between artist and audience. According to Leon Trotsky, literary form has a high degree of autonomy. It evolves partly in accordance with its own internal pressures and does not always bend to every ideological view that shapes up. Form, for Trotsky, is always a complex unity of three elements: it is partly shaped by a relatively autonomous literary history of forms; it takes shape out of certain dominant ideological structures and it embodies a specific set of relations between the author and the audience. Eagleton asserts that it is this dialectical unity between these elements that Marxist Criticism is concerned with. It is in the work of Georg Lukacs that the problem of literary forms and their inherent ideologies have been most thoroughly dealt with. For Lukacs, a great artist is one who can recapture and recreate a harmonious complex totality of human life by combating the dualistic framework of a capitalistic society. Lukacs calls such art 'realism', which merges a complex set of relations between man and nature with what is typical about a significant phase of history. He further states that it is the historical content, which lays the basis for their formal achievement. He says the richness and depth of created characters depend upon the richness and depth of the total social process. For the French Critic, Pierre Machery, literary work is tied to ideology. He says that in order to expose a text's ideology, we must focus on what the text does not say and not on what it says. He argues that it is in the silences, gaps etc that the presence of ideology can be felt. He further states that a literary work is incomplete and displays a conflict of meanings. The significance of a work lies not in the unity but in the difference between these meanings. Thus, literary work for Machery, is always 'de-centred' – no central essence to it, just a continuous conflict and discrepancy of meanings.

Chapter III – The Writer and Commitment

In the 1930s, state began to exercise direct control over literature and arts and a new hardline code was imposed, based on the writings of Lenin rather than those of Marx and Engels. Lenin had argued in 1905 that literature must become an instrument of the party: "Literature must become a cog and a screw of one single great democratic machine". His literary interests confined on the whole to an admiration of 'realism', to be specific, social realism. Trotsky agrees with Lenin when he insists on the need for social culture and when he recognizes that artistic form is the product of social content. But he differs when he ascribes a high degree of autonomy to literary work. Marx and Engels stress on necessary freedom of art from direct political determinism. Their attitude to the question of commitment of writer is best revealed in two famous letters written by Engels to novelists who had submitted their work to him for perusal. In his letter to Minna Kautsky (1885), Engels criticized her for an openly partisan attitude towards a political tendency and thereby the propagandist nature of her work. In a second letter of 1888 to Margaret Harkness, he criticizes her work for failing to integrate any sense of the historical role and development in her depiction of the working class. Engels' two letters clearly suggest that overt political commitment in fiction is unnecessary as truly realist writing will itself dramatize the significant forces of social life.

The question of 'committed' literature remained unresolved because of confusion among the English Marxist critics. Much of English Marxist Criticism seem to agree to the view of art as the passive reflection of the economic base and to a romantic belief in art as projecting an ideal world and leading men to new values. This contradiction is clearly marked in the work of Christopher Caudwel whose idea of art's relation to reality is an efficient channeling of social energies on the one hand and a utopian dream on the other. Alick West in Crisis and Criticism (1937) also sees art as a way of organizing social energy and that the writer awakens in the readers similar energies. Further, in the discussion of ideology and aesthetics, several Marxist critics consider aesthetic as a mere secondary matter of style and technique. This finds expression in Lukacs The Historical Novel, which Eagleton quotes: "It does not matter whether Scott or Manzoni were aesthetically superior to, say Heinrich Mann, or at least this is not the main point. What is important is that Scott and Manzoni, Pushkin and Tolstoy were able to grasp and portray popular life in a more profound, authentic human and concretely historical fashion than even the most outstanding writers of our day …".

Eagleton disagrees with Lukacs and several Marxists on the above point and argues that the adjectives used by Lukacs to portray popular life make what is meant by 'aesthetically superior'.

Chapter IV – The Author as Producer

Eagleton states that literature may be a product of social consciousness, a world vision but it is also an industry: books are also commodities produced by publishers and sold at the market for a profit. The Marxist critics understood the fact that art is a form of social production. Terry Eagleton explicates his views, drawing from the views of Walter Benjamin and Bertolt Brecht. He says that these Marxist critics see literature as a form of social and economic production, which exists alongside and interrelates with other such forms. According to Benjamin, art depends upon certain techniques of production, which are part of the stage of development of artistic production and they involve a set of relations between the artist and his audience. In Marxism, the stage is set for revolution when the productive forces and productive relations enter into contradiction with each other. Benjamin, in his essay, "The Author as Producer" (1934) applies this theory to art itself. He states that an artist should not merely accept the old, existing modes of artistic production but should transform and revolutionize those forces: its purpose is not putting forward a message through existing media but it is a question of revolutionizing the media themselves. Cinema, Photography, Music, Literature etc not only alter the traditional technique and relations of artistic production but they continuously modify traditional modes of perception.

Brecht's 'Epic Theatre' exemplifies Benjamin's theory of revolutionary art as one, which changes the modes, rather than the contents of artistic production. Brecht succeeds in altering the functional relations between stage and audience, text and producer, producer and actor. Subverting the traditional theatre with its illusion of reality, Brecht produced a new kind of drama with its base on 'Alienation Effect'. This helps to distance the audience from the performance so that they can be prevented from identifying emotionally with the play and maintain its power of critical judgement. It also persuades the audience to question the attitudes and behaviour, which was accepted as 'natural'.

Eagleton deals with three interrelated aspects of revolutionary art – the new meaning it gives to the idea of form, its redefinition of the author and its redefinition of the artistic product itself. He argues that form announces modes of ideological perception and embodies a certain set of productive relations between artists and audiences. He agrees with Brecht, Benjamin and Machery when they consider the author as primarily a producer and not a creator. He states that the artist uses certain means of production (techniques of live art) to transform the materials of language and experience into a determinate product. In assessing the question of the nature of the artwork itself, Eagleton echoes Brecht in stating that a work should not be completed in itself but like any social product should be completed only in the act of being used.

Both Brecht and Eagleton here only emphasize Marx's view that a product fully becomes a product through consumption. Eagleton also addresses the Marxist debate on realism and modernism. He diffuses oppositional ideologies in them and opines that realism could be extended to include modernist techniques as seen in Brecht.

Eagleton also alerts the readers of 'technologism,' that is, art forms being trapped in the technical forces that could change the mode of production and the experience of art.

Conclusion:

Terry Eagleton upholds in his Marxism and Literary Criticism the traditional Marxist view that literature is a part of historical process. However, he also includes in his consideration of literature the Neo-Marxist tolerance for formal experiments and Modernism.

Block-6 Feminist Theories

Feminism is considered as an organized movement, which promotes equality for men and women in political, economic and social spheres. Feminists, in general, believe that women are oppressed mainly due to their gender in the dominant ideology or patriarchy. Patriarchy is a system, which oppresses women through its social, economic, political institutions and cultural practices. Men, to maintain greater power over women have created boundaries and obstacles for women. Patriarchy also perpetuates the oppression of minorities and homosexuals. Various schools of Feminism like Radical Feminism; Liberal Feminism, Cultural Feminism and Socialist Feminism have advocated drastic changes in the power relation between men and women.

XXIII

Introduction to Feminist Theories

Scan for the video

Feminist theory is an extension of Feminism that tries to interrogate gender bias through theoretical engagement.

Feminist theories have developed largely under three main categories:

a. Theories having an essentialist focus, which include Psychoanalytic Feminism.

b. Theories aimed at defining and establishing a feminist literary canon or theories seeking to re-interpret and re-vision literature, culture and history. This branch includes Gynocriticism and Liberal Feminism.

c. Theories focusing on sexual difference and sexual politics. This group includes Gender Studies, Lesbian Studies, Cultural Feminism, Socialist Feminism and Queer Theory.

Simon De Beauvoir's study, **The Second Sex,** is generally considered to be the origin of feminist literary theory. Though Beauvoir's work is attacked for a flawed perception of her own body politics, it is nevertheless considered as a ground breaking book of feminist theory that interrogates the 'othering' of women by Western philosophy. However, merely unearthing women's literature did not ensure a prominent place for feminist theory. Hence, subsequent feminist theories were engaged in assessing and questioning number of preconceptions inherent in a literary canon dominated by male beliefs. Betty Friedan's The Feminist Mystique (1963), Kate Millet's Sexual Politics (1970), Judith Fetterley's The Resisting Reader (1978), Elaine Showalter's Literature of Their Own (1977) and Sandra Gilbert and Susan Gubar's Mad Woman in the Attic (1979) are just a handful of many critiques that question cultural, sexual intellectual and / or psychological stereotypes about women.

XXIV

A Vindication of the Rights of Women by Mary Wollstonecraft.

Scan for the video

Mary Wollstonecraft

Q.1 Examine Mary Wollstonecraft's contribution to Women's right and their education.

Ans.

Introduction:

A Vindication of the Rights of Women is a book-length feminist essay by British writer Mary Wollstonecraft, published in 1792. She was English writer and passionate advocate of educational and social equality for women.

She outlined her beliefs in A Vindication of the Rights of Woman (1792), considered a classic of feminism. Her mature work on woman's place in society is A Vindication of the Rights of Woman (1792), which calls for women and men to be educated equally.

Wollstonecraft's work was unique in suggesting that the betterment of women's status be affected through such political change as the radical reform of national educational systems. Such change, she concluded, would benefit all society.

A Vindication of the Rights of Women:'

Wollstonecraft was encouraged to write this text after reading a French clergyman and leading diplomat Charles Maurice de Talleyrand-Perigord's 1791 report to Rights of Women the French National Assembly. In 1791, he submitted the Report on Public Education to the French National Assembly as a part of the process of revising the French Constitution. This report only addressed public education to men; and stated that women should only receive a domestic education as it was deserved sufficient for women. Wollstonecraft was disappointed by such proposals of the report regarding women's education in France.

In the Rights of Woman, Wollstonecraft responded to those education and political theorists and philosophers of the 18th century who believed that women should not receive a rational education

- A Vindication of the Rights of Women called for female equality, particularly in the area of education. Wollstonecraft dismissed the cultivation of traditional female virtues of submission and service and argued that women could not be good mothers, good wives and good household managers if they were not well-educated. She claimed that women were expected to spend too much time on maintaining their delicate appearance and gentle demeanor, sacrificing intelligence for beauty and becoming flower-like playthings for men.
- The book is divided into thirteen chapters, in which Wollstonecraft addressed topics such as the importance of educating women equally, treating women with dignity and providing women with the proper training to be good wives and mothers and intelligent companions for their husbands.
- Wollstonecraft argued, could women teach and raise children and run a household if they focused only on their own appearance and on minor accomplishments like speaking French prettily, playing the piano and drawing? Such accomplishments made a woman desirable to a man as an amusement, but not as an equal companion.
- Wollstonecraft examines the writings and viewpoints of her contemporaries. She illustrates how thinkers such as Rousseau impose a debasing stereotype upon women by suggesting that their sole purpose is "to please the man". She also criticizes the concept of women having rules of "decorum" to follow, which wouldn't teach them to intelligently decide between right and wrong, but simply to blindly obey.

Conclusion:

Mary Wollstonecraft went further than her contemporaries in late eighteenth-century England by demanding that the twin values of reason and revolution which they cherished be applied to the cause of women's education. Given that the association of ideas shapes individual identity Wollstonecraft argues that education is essential to train the minds of women away from enslavement to early impressions. She highlights the inferiority of contemporary literature and life to show that defective education of women is the cause of social and personal ills. Wollstonecraft's work is typical of its age and culture. It illustrates the nexus between early socialism and feminism but ultimately seems to demand equality for women mainly as a means to, an end - that of the companionate marriage -rather than as an end in itself.

XXV

A Room of One's Own by Verginia Woolf

Scan for the video

Adeline Verginia Woolf

Q.1 Comment on the significance of the title *The Second Sex.*

Q.2 Evaluate Virginia Woolf as a feminist critic.

Ans.

Introduction:

Adeline Verginia Woolf was an English writer, considered one of the most important modernist 20th century authors and a pioneer in the use of stream of consciousness as a narrative device.

She was an important writer in the field of feminism and she indited her work called A Room One's Own in 1929.

This work is accepted as a basic beginning texts of feminist criticism.

The work is based on two lectures delivered in October 1928 at Newnham College and Girton College, women's constituent colleges at the University of Cambridge.

In her essay Woolf uses metaphors to explore social injustice and comment on women's lack of free expression.

Her metaphor of a fish explains her most essential point "A women must have money and a room of her own if she is to write fiction.

A Room One's Own. (Analysis)

- In essay, A Room of One's Own, Virginia Woolf attempt to uncover the pervading patriarchal ideology that deprives women of most of the opportunities to enjoy life as freely and confidently as men.
- In her exploration of this idea, Woolf launches a number of provocative sociological and aesthetic critiques. She reviews not only the state of women's own literature, but also the state of scholarship, both theoretical and historical, concerning women. She also elaborates an aesthetics based on the principle of "incandescence," the ideal state in which everything that is merely personal is consumed in the intensity and truth of one's art.
- Consisting of 6 chapters A Room of One's Own, is a seminal work that contains writing that covers a wide area and exposes the male privilege and the way women have been excluded from the mainstream of life; how they are cornered from the cultural, social and economic life of the society.
- In fact, the said book seems to have been intended as a commentary on the social disabilities that have prevented women from realizing their productive and creative possibilities.

Husband/ Father's property excluded woman.

In the first chapter of A Room of One's Own, she concentrates on the mechanism that makes women powerless by not allowing them to use her husband's or father's property.

A woman cannot spend a single penny on her own will, she even cannot use her own money without her husbands or father's consent.

It is not a woman but her husband who decide how and where her money is to be spent.

Women deprived of certain experience and opportunities that men have.

She reflects on various differences and discriminations as "Why did men drink wine and women water? Why was women sex so prosperous and the other so poor?

She probes into the fact that why women are the center of attraction for almost all the men. Why there are innumerable books, articles and essays on women by men who have no more qualification then that they are men.

She also muses why men are so envious of an angry with women and conclude that it is men's sense of insecurity of losing power and sense of male superiority that makes them jealous and angry when a patriarch insist on.

Chapter 2

Searching for answers to the questions she posed about men, women, wealth, and creativity, the narrator explores the British Museum in London. She soon realizes there are too many books written about women almost all by men for her to digest them all. On the other hand, there are hardly any books by women on men. She wonders why there is such a great disparity, and randomly selects a dozen books. Trying to come up with an answer for why women are poor, she locates a multitude of other topics on women in the books, and a contradictory array of men's opinions on women. Frustrated, she unwittingly draws a picture of an unattractive, angry-looking professor at work on one of the books about the inferiority of women. It occurs to her that she has become angry because the professor has written angrily himself. Had he written "dispassionately," she would have paid more attention to his argument, and not to him. After her anger dissipates, she wonders why these men are all angry. She returns the books, finding them useless, and goes to lunch.

Condition of Women – Voiceless and identity less.

In the third chapter of A Room of One's Own, Woolf centers her attention on the condition of women. She meditates on the extent a woman is dependent on the will of the male members of the family, what a voiceless and identity less creature she is and how she is compelled to sacrifice her interest for the well of the male relatives.

Woman cannot dare to pen down her actual feelings on paper.

In the fourth chapter, Woolf throws light on how a woman is discouraged in any efforts to do or say somethings.

Deprived of all the privileges, support, encouragement, a woman cannot dare to pen down her actual feelings on paper.

Woolf compares Shakespeare and Jane Austen and finds the latter no less talented. "Jane Austen pervades every word that she wrote and so does Shakespeare.

If Jane Austen suffered in any way from her circumstances, it was in the narrowness of life that was imposed up on her. Her life was narrow because she was a woman who had to pass much of a time within her house and she could not wander as freely and frequently as Shakespeare did.

Women should get a room of her own and money.

In the 5ᵗʰ chapter, Woolf again concentrates on women's writing, she maintains that a woman should violates all the established rule to assert her identity.

She further said women can write freely and frankly only if she is independent economically and mentally.

Woolf meditates....

.... Give her room of her own and 500 a year, let her speak a mind and leave out half that she now puts in, and she will write a better book one of these days.

Man – Womanly and Woman manly. (Chapter 6)

Woolf tried to illustrate that if writers want to create a good writing, he or she need to be looking at other either man or woman side.

Similarly, as previous chapters, instead of blame on man blindly, Woolf give out a fair point that both man and woman should think man-womanly or woman-manly in order to make permanent literature.

Conclusion:

It can therefore, the argued that Virginia Woolf speculated on so many problems concerning women a century earlier, which few feminists' critic could have done after her.

Woolf did not think only about the problems women faced in her time or before her, but she had a power to anticipate and see other problems that were beyond her time that woman will have to face.

XXVI
Modern Fiction by Verginia Woolf

Scan for the video

Introduction:

Virginia Woolf (1882-1941) an English novelist and critic who made an original contribution to English Novel. Modern fiction is an essay by Virginia Woolf. This essay was written in 1919 but published in 1921 with a series of short stories called Monday or Tuesday.

The essay is the criticism of writers and literature from the previous generation. It also acts as a guide for writers of modern fiction to write what they feel, not what society or publisher want them to write.

Virginia Woolf's "Modern Fiction" details how modern fictional writers and authors should write what inspires them and not to follow any special method. She believed that Writers are constrained by the publishing business, by what society believes literature should look like and what society has dictated how literature should be written. Woolf believed it is a writer's Job to write the complexities in life, the unknown, not the important things.

Modern fiction is one of the most effective seminar essays in criticism which makes a clear break of modern fiction from the Victorian novel. Mrs. Woolf first traces the progress of the novel from its beginning in the 18th Century. But she traces it on basis of the philosophy of evaluation in general. According to her, the earlier novelists really did what they actually could within their limited means. With their simple tools and primitive materials, it might be said "Fielding did well and Jane Austen even better."

She criticises M.G. Wells, Arnold Benett, John Galsworthy of writing about unimportant things and called them materialists. According to her, they put life into their novels. They are mainly concerned with the body, not the soul of the novel. This is particularly because they are all materialists and are concerned with fixities not with movements.

While Woolf criticizes these three authors, she praises several other authors for their innovation. This group of writers she name spiritualists, and include James Joyce who Woolf says writes what interests and move him.

Woolf wanted writers to focus on the awkwardness of life and craved originality in their work. Writers need to turn away from the material and instead embrace what she calls the 'spiritual' in order to make fiction new and relevant.

Mrs. Woolf make it clear that the objective of the writer in his or her creation is to look within and life as a whole. The traditionalism or materialism do not capture at that moment. Thus to trust upon life, a writer is free and he could write what he chose.

To sum up, Virginia Woolf observes that "Nothing-no method, un experiment, even of the wildest-is forbidden, but only falsity and pretence." "the proper stuff of fiction does not exist, everything is the proper stuff of fiction, every feeling, every thought, every quality of brain & spirit is drawn upon."

Conclusion:

Woolf's "Modern Fiction" essay focuses on how writers should write or what she hopes for them to write. She does not suggest a specific way to write. instead a she wants writers to simple write what interests them in any way that they choose to write. She suggests "Any method is right, every method is right, that expresses what we wish to express, if we are writers, that brings us closer to the novelists" intension if we are readers." She wanted writers to express themselves in such a way that it showed life. She set out to inspire writers of modern fiction by calling for originality, criticizing those who focused on the unimportant things and comparing the differences of cultural authors, all for the sake of fiction and literature.

XXVII

Gynocriticism by Elaine Showalter

Scan for the video

Elaine Showalter

Q.1 Explain the term Gynocriticism.

Ans.

Introduction:

This term was first used by Elaine Showalter in her essay, "Towards a Feminist Poetics" (1979). It indicates woman as a writer, as a producer of textual meaning. Gynocriticism is considered as a branch of Feminism concerned with developing a specifically female framework for dealing with works of women. Gynocriticism aims to develop woman-centred tools to understand production, motivation, analysis and interpretation in all literary forms including journals and letters. Further, it also tries to identify feminine subject matters in literature written by women in an attempt to uncover in literary history a female tradition. Showalter argues that there is a distinctive feminine mode of experience, thinking, evaluation and self-perception. Her objective was to develop female aesthetics.

Showalter says that there is no term in English or literary theory to describe a discourse that specializes in history, themes, genres and structures of literature by women. She also spells out the concerns of Gynocriticism as follows:

1. To identify what are taken to be the distinct feminine subject matters in literature written by women.

2. To uncover in literary history, a female tradition.

3. To see how women writers emulate and find support in earlier women writers who, in turn, give emotional support to their own readers and successors.

4. To show that there is a distinctive feminine mode of experiencing subjectivity.

5. To specify the traits of a woman's language, that is, woman's style of speech, writing, sentence construction and discourse. Showalter explains in her essay the scope and objectives of Gynocritics:

Gynocritics is related to feminist research in history, anthropology, psychology and sociology, all of which have developed hypotheses of a female subculture including not only the ascribed status and the internalized constructs of femininity, but also the occupations, interactions and consciousness of women.

Showalter also defines the parameters and concerns of Gynocritics She says that it is concerned with women as producers of textual meaning and "Its subjects include the psychodynamics of female creativity, linguistics and the problems of female language; the trajectory of the individual or collective female literary career, literary history, and of course, studies of particular writers and works.

XXVIII

FEMINIST CRITICISM IN THE WILDERNESS
by Elaine Showalter

Scan for the video

Introduction:

The essay by Elaine Showalter is an attempt to study the field of literary criticism from the feminist point of view. Showalter has tried to study the various aspects of feminist criticism while also pointing out the aims it should be trying to attain, the problems it faces and the reasons for these problems.

The essay considers the fact that like feminist creative writers, feminist critics also face certain obstacles which have got highlighted after the rise of feminism. Showalter has tried to analyze in detail the belief that feminist criticism is in wilderness, which means, feminist critics are not capable enough to produce coherent speculations.

1. Pluralism and the Feminist Critique

Showalter begins this essay by pointing out a dialogue by Carolyn Heilbrun and Catherine Stimpson. They had pointed out that two poles were identifiable in feminist literary criticism- one concentrating on the errors of the past and the other focus on the beauty of imagination. Both these aspects contribute in removing the effects of 'female servitude' that has existed in the society since ages. She also quotes Matthew Arnold to state that criticism, as a process, has to pass through a stage of wilderness to reach at the desired standards. Then, taking support from Geoffrey Hartman's quote, she forwards the belief that all criticism, and not only feminist criticism, is in wilderness. Analyzing one of the reasons for this, so called, wilderness in feminist criticism, she clarifies that the reason is lack of an exclusive theoretical framework for feminist criticism. It is always seen in association with some other strategy and, therefore, fails to work consistently. For instance, feminist critics supporting Marxism treat feminist criticism differently than those opposing racism.

An early obstacle in establishment of the above mentioned theoretical framework was the inability of many women to respond to the demand of openness required for the success of feminist criticism. In some aspects of society, women had been locked out and in some others they had been locked in. they were not allowed to participate in some aspects of social interaction and forced to participate in some others. Thus, some believed feminism to be equivalent to opposition to the establish canons.

Showalter says that what seemed to be 'a theoretical impasse' was actually an evolutionary phase. During this stage, feminist criticism moved on from the stage of awakening to the stage marked by 'anxiety about the isolation of feminist criticism from a critical community'. The definition of feminist criticism with reference to other feminist theories has been a serious debate and feminist critics have been unable to address this issue. They fail to understand the need to think beyond their own beliefs as well and to communicate with the systems they wish to change. Although feminist critics have communicated with these systems but the communication has been unclear being based entirely on the media of feminist critics.

There are two modes of feminist criticism. Showalter calls the first one 'feminist reading' or 'feminist critique'. It is concerned to the reading of texts to understand the image of woman in literature and to work out the beliefs and stereotypes concerned to woman highlighted and publicized by literary texts. This is a mode of interpretation and has been quite influential in decoding the relationship of women to literature.

Showalter points out that feminist criticism is revisionist being dependent on male creative theory, i.e. the creative works and interpretations produced on the basis of male experience. Feminist critics try to analyze and respond to male creative theory. This need to be changed to achieve feminist criticism that is 'women centred, independent and intellectually coherent'.

2. Defining the Feminine: Gynocritics and the Woman's Text

It is well accepted that a woman's writing would always be feminine but defining 'feminine' has always been a problem. The second mode of feminist criticism concentrates on this definition. It analyzes women as writers. It undertakes the study of 'history, styles, themes, genres, and structures of writing by women'. It also studies in details the various aspects of female creativity and female literary tradition. Showalter has coined the term 'gynocritics' for the 'specialized critical discourse' that uses women's writings as its exclusive subject. However, identifying the unique elements of women's writings is again a problem. French Feminist Criticism has identified the influence of female body on female language and texts. However, the issue has been approached towards differently in different countries. Four basic models of difference are being used most commonly- biological, linguistic, psychoanalytic and cultural. Each of these models is like a school of gynocentric feminist criticism and has its own preferences for texts, methods and beliefs.

3. Women's Writing and Woman's Body

It is one of the clearest statements of gender difference. Theories like that of better developed frontal lobes in case of males and of the use of 20 percent of creative energy for physiological functions in case of women have been used in the past to advocate the superiority of men over women. Many critics have associated the act of creation of text to the generative process which only male used to be considered capable of undertaking.

The metaphor of literary paternity used to be associated to penis and, thus, to male. Showalter, however, associates it to womb comparing literary creativity to childbirth. The level and implication of the mention of anatomy in text by male and female writers, respectively, has also been different. However, study of biological imagery in women's writings could be helpful only when other factors affecting them are also kept in mind.

4. Women's Writing and Women's Language

This concept analyzes if men and women use language differently while creating texts. It studies if factors like biology, social preferences and cultural beliefs could affect the language of a gender. It also considers the concept of 'the oppressor's language', the use of language by men to dominate women. For woman, the popular language could be like a foreign language which she is unable to be comfortable with. So, there is a call for development of separate feminine language. However, the irony is that even in communities where women are believed to have developed a separate language, their language is marked by secrecy.

The differences in male and female speech in terms of 'speech, intonation and language use' are the most obvious examples of difference in man's and woman's language. Feminist criticism should, most importantly, work for providing women an access to language so that a wide range of words is available to them. Language is sufficient enough to give expression to women's consciousness only if she is not denied access to all the resources of language.

5. Women's Writing and Woman's Psyche

This aspect deals with the connection between author's psyche and creative process in general. The difference in creative process in case of a male and a female is then studied on the basis of this connection. Various psychological theories have suggested that female is inferior in terms of creative capabilities. Critics have been trying to establish new principles of feminist psychoanalysis which would try to differentiate gender identities rather than following Freudian theories. Certain common emotional dimensions could be identified in texts of women writers belonging to different countries.

6. Women's Writing and Women's Culture

The theory of culture as a factor affecting women's writing is inclusive of the theories of biology, language and psyche. The influence of all these factors is guided by the cultural situation of a woman. History has not included female experience. Thus, history is inadequate to understand women's experience. Woman's culture is not a sub-culture of main culture. They are part of general culture itself. If patriarchal society applies restraints on them, they transform it into complementarity. Thus, women experience duality of culture including general culture and women's culture. Women form 'muted group' in society and men form 'dominant group'. Ardener suggested a diagram with two circles representing these two groups respectively. All language of the dominant group is all acceptable language. So, the muted group has to follow the same language. The part of the circle representing the muted group which does not coincide with the other circle represents that part of women's life which has not found any expression in history. It represents the activities, experiences and feelings of women which are unknown to men. Since they do not form part of men's life, they do not get representation in history. This 'female zone' is also known as 'wild zone' since it is out of the range of dominant boundary. Women could not write on experiences belonging exclusively on the wild zone. They have to give representation to the dominant culture in their texts. There are other muted groups as well than women. For instance, literary identity of a black American poet is forced upon her by the trends of the dominant group.

Feminist critics try to identify the aspects of women writers which do not follow the trends established by the male writers. For instance, Woolf's works show tendencies other than those of modernism. However, these tendencies are visible in the sections which have so far been considered obscure or imperfect. Feminist critics should attempt 'thick description' of women's writings. It is possible only when effect of gender and female literary tradition are considered among the various factors that affect the meaning of the text.

Conclusion: Showalter concludes that the 'promised land' or situation when there would be no difference in the texts written by man and woman could not be attained. Attainment of that situation should not be the aim of feminist critics.

XXIX

The Second Sex by Simone De Beauvoir

Scan for the video

Simone de Beauvoir

Introduction:

The Second Sex is a 1949 book by the French existentialist philosopher Simone de Beauvoir, in which the author discusses the treatment of women in the present society as well as throughout all of history. Beauvoir researched and wrote the book in about 14 months between 1946 and 1949. She published the work in two volumes: Facts and Myths, and Lived Experience. Some chapters first appeared in the journal Les Temps modernes.

One of Beauvoir's best-known and controversial books (banned by the Vatican), The Second Sex is regarded as a groundbreaking work of feminist philosophy, and as the starting inspiration point of second-wave feminism.

Analysis of the Second Sex:

Volume One

1. Beauvoir asks, "What is woman?"She argues that man is considered the default, while woman is considered the "Other": "Thus, humanity is male, and man defines woman not herself, but as relative to him." Beauvoir describes the relationship of ovum to sperm in various creatures (fish,

insects, mammals), leading up to the human being. She describes women's subordination to the species in terms of reproduction, compares the physiology of men and women, concluding that values cannot be based on physiology and that the facts of biology must be viewed in light of the ontological, economic, social, and physiological context.

2. According to Beauvoir, two factors explain the evolution of women's condition: participation in production, and freedom from reproductive slavery. Beauvoir writes that motherhood left woman "riveted to her body", like an animal, and made it possible for men to dominate her and Nature. She describes man's gradual domination of women, starting with the statue of a female Great Goddess found in Susa, and eventually the opinion of ancient Greeks like Pythagoras, who wrote, "There is a good principle that created order, light, and man and a bad principle that created chaos, darkness, and woman." Men succeed in the world by transcendence, but immanence is the lot of women. Beauvoir writes that men oppress women when they seek to perpetuate the family and keep patrimony intact. She compares women's situation in ancient Greece with Rome. In Greece, with exceptions like Sparta, where there were no restraints on women's freedom, women were treated almost like slaves. In Rome, because men were still the masters, women enjoyed more rights, but, still discriminated against on the basis of their sex, had only empty freedom.

Discussing Christianity, Beauvoir argues that, with the exception of the German tradition, it and its clergy have served to subordinate women. She also describes prostitution and the changes in dynamics brought about by courtly love that occurred about the twelfth century. Beauvoir describes, from the early fifteenth century, "great Italian ladies and courtesans", and singles out the Spaniard Teresa of Ávila as successfully raising "herself as high as a man". Through the nineteenth century, women's legal status remained unchanged, but individuals (like Marguerite de Navarre) excelled by writing and acting. Some men helped women's status through their works. Beauvoir finds fault with the Napoleonic Code, criticizes Auguste Comte and Honoré de Balzac, and describes Pierre-Joseph Proudhon as an anti-feminist. The Industrial Revolution of the nineteenth century gave women an escape from their homes, but they were paid little for their work. Beauvoir traces the growth of trade unions and participation by women. She examines the spread of birth control methods and the history of abortion. Beauvoir relates the history of women's suffrage, and writes that women like Rosa Luxemburg and Marie Curie "brilliantly demonstrate that it is not women's inferiority that has determined their historical insignificance: It is their historical insignificance that has doomed them to inferiority".

Beauvoir provides a presentation about the "everlasting disappointment" of women, for the most part from a male heterosexual's point of view. She covers female menstruation, virginity, and female sexuality, including copulation, marriage, motherhood, and prostitution. To illustrate man's experience of the "horror of feminine fertility", Beauvoir quotes the British Medical Journal of 1878 in which a member of the British Medical Association writes, "It is an indisputable fact that meat goes bad when touched by menstruating women." She quotes poetry by André Breton, Léopold Sédar Senghor, Michel Leiris, Paul Verlaine, Edgar Allan Poe, Paul Valéry, Johann Wolfgang von Goethe, and William Shakespeare, along with other novels, philosophers, and films. Beauvoir writes that sexual division is maintained in homosexuality.

Examining the work of Henry de Montherlant, D. H. Lawrence, Paul Claudel, André Breton, and Stendhal, Beauvoir writes that these "examples show that the great collective myths are reflected in each singular writer". "Feminine devotion is demanded as a duty by Montherlant and Lawrence; less arrogant, Claudel, Breton, and Stendhal admire it as a generous choice..."She finds that woman is "the privileged Other", that Other is defined in the "way the One chooses to posit himself", and writes that, "But the only earthly destiny reserved to the woman equal, child-woman, soul sister, woman-sex, and female animal is always man. "Beauvoir writes that, "The absence or insignificance of the female element in a body of work is symptomatic... It loses importance in a period like ours in which each individual's particular problems are of secondary import."

Beauvoir writes that "mystery" is prominent among men's myths about women. She also writes that mystery is not confined by sex to women, but, instead, by situation, and that it pertains to any slave. She thinks it disappeared during the eighteenth century when men, however briefly, considered women to be peers. She quotes Arthur Rimbaud, who writes that, hopefully, one day, women can become fully human beings when man gives her her freedom.

Volume Two

Presenting a child's life beginning with birth,Beauvoir contrasts a girl's upbringing with a boy's, who at age 3 or 4 is told he is a "little man". A girl is taught to be a woman and her "feminine" destiny is imposed on her by society. She has no innate "maternal instinct". A girl comes to believe in and to worship a male god and to create imaginary adult lovers. The discovery of sex is a "phenomenon as painful as weaning" and she views it with disgust. When she discovers that men, not women, are the masters of the world this "imperiously modifies her consciousness of herself". Beauvoir describes puberty, the beginning of menstruation, and the way girls imagine sex with a man. She relates several ways that girls in their late teens accept their "femininity", which may include running away from home, fascination with the disgusting, following nature, or stealing. Beauvoir describes sexual relations with men, maintaining that the repercussions of the first of these experiences informs a woman's whole life. Beauvoir describes women's sexual relations with women. She writes that "homosexuality is no more a deliberate perversion than a fatal curse".

Beauvoir writes that "to ask two spouses bound by practical, social and moral ties to satisfy each other sexually for their whole lives is pure absurdity". She describes the work of married women, including housecleaning, writing that it is "holding away death but also refusing life". She thinks, "what makes the lot of the wife-servant ungratifying is the division of labor that dooms her wholly to the general and inessential". Beauvoir writes that a woman finds her dignity only in accepting her vassalage which is bed "service" and housework "service". A woman is weaned away from her family and finds only "disappointment" on the day after her wedding. Beauvoir points out various inequalities between a wife and husband whom find themselves in a threesome and finds they pass the time not in love but in "conjugal love". She thinks that marriage "almost always destroys woman". She quotes Sophia Tolstoy who wrote in her diary: "you are stuck there forever and there you must sit". Beauvoir thinks marriage is a perverted institution oppressing both men and women.

In Beauvoir's view, abortions performed legally by doctors would have little risk to the mother. She argues that the Catholic Church cannot make the claim that the souls of the unborn would not end up in heaven because of their lack of baptism because that would be contradictory to other Church teachings. She writes that the issue of abortion is not an issue of morality but of "masculine sadism" toward woman. Beauvoir describes pregnancy, which is viewed as both a gift and a curse to woman. In this new creation of a new life the woman loses herself, seeing herself as "no longer anything ... [but] a passive instrument". Beauvoir writes that, "maternal sadomasochism creates guilt feelings for the daughter that will express themselves in sadomasochistic behavior toward her own children, without end", and makes an appeal for socialist child rearing practices.

Beauvoir describes a woman's clothes, her girlfriends and her relationships with men. She writes that "marriage, by frustrating women's erotic satisfaction, denies them the freedom and individuality of their feelings, drives them to adultery". Beauvoir describes prostitutes and their relationships with pimps and with other women, as well as hetaeras. In contrast to prostitutes, hetaeras can gain recognition as an individual and if successful can aim higher and be publicly distinguished. Beauvoir writes that women's path to menopause might arouse woman's homosexual feelings (which Beauvoir thinks are latent in most women). When she agrees to grow old she becomes elderly with half of her adult life left to live. A woman might choose to live through her children (often her son) or her grandchildren but she faces "solitude, regret, and ennui". To pass her time she might engage in useless "women's handiwork", watercolors, music or reading, or she might join charitable organizations. While a few rare women are committed to a cause and have an end in mind, Beauvoir concludes that "the highest form of freedom a woman-parasite can have is stoic defiance or skeptical irony".

According to Beauvoir, while a woman knows how to be as active, effective and silent as a man, her situation keeps her being useful, preparing food, clothes, and lodging. She worries because she does not do anything, she complains, she cries, and she may threaten suicide. She protests but doesn't escape her lot. She may achieve happiness in "Harmony" and the "Good" as illustrated by Virginia Woolf and Katherine Mansfield. Beauvoir thinks it is pointless to try to decide whether a woman is superior or inferior, and that it is obvious that the man's situation is "infinitely preferable". She writes, "for woman there is no other way out than to work for her liberation".

Beauvoir describes narcissistic women, who might find themselves in a mirror and in the theater, and women in and outside marriage: "The day when it will be possible for the woman to love in her strength and not in her weakness, not to escape from herself but to find herself, not out of resignation but to affirm herself, love will become for her as for man the source of life and not a mortal danger." Beauvoir discusses the lives of several women, some of whom developed stigmata. Beauvoir writes that these women may develop a relation "with an unreal: her double or god; or she creates an unreal relation with a real being...". She also mentions women with careers who are able to escape sadism and masochism. A few women have successfully reached a state of equality, and Beauvoir, in a footnote, singles out the example of Clara and Robert Schumann. Beauvoir says that the goals of wives can be overwhelming: as a wife tries to be elegant, a good housekeeper and a good mother. Singled out are "actresses, dancers and singers" who may achieve independence. Among writers, Beauvoir chooses only Emily Brontë, Woolf and ("sometimes") Mary Webb (and she mentions Colette and Mansfield) as among those who have tried to approach nature "in its inhuman freedom". Beauvoir then says that women don't "challenge the human condition" and that in comparison to the few "greats", a woman comes out as "mediocre" and will continue at that level for quite some time. A woman could not have been Vincent van Gogh or Franz Kafka. Beauvoir thinks that perhaps, of all women, only Saint Teresa lived her life for herself. She says it is "high time" a woman "be left to take her own chances".

Conclusion: In her conclusion, Beauvoir looks forward to a future when women and men are equals, something the "Soviet revolution promised" but did not ever deliver. She concludes that, "to carry off this supreme victory, men and women must, among other things and beyond their natural differentiations, unequivocally affirm their brotherhood.

Block -7 Deconstruction

Deconstruction involves the close reading of texts in order to demonstrate that any given text has irreconcilably contradictory meanings, rather than being a unified, logical whole. As J. Hillis Miller, the preeminent American deconstructionist, has explained in an essay entitled Stevens' Rock and Criticism as Cure (1976), "Deconstruction is not a dismantling of the structure of a text, but a demonstration that it has already dismantled itself. Its apparently solid ground is no rock but thin air."

XXX

Introduction to Deconstruction

Scan for the video

Deconstruction was both created and has been profoundly influenced by the French philosopher Jacques Derrida. Derrida, who coined the term deconstruction, argues that in Western culture, people tend to think and express their thoughts in terms of binary oppositions (white / black, masculine / feminine, cause /effect, conscious /unconscious, presence / absence, speech writing). Derrida suggests these oppositions are hierarchies in miniature, containing one term that Western culture views as positive or superior and another considered negative or inferior, even if only slightly so. Through deconstruction, Derrida aims to erase the boundary between binary oppositions—and to do so in such a way that the hierarchy implied by the oppositions is thrown into question.

Although its ultimate aim may be to criticize Western logic, deconstruction arose as a response to structuralism and formalism. Structuralists believed that all elements of human culture, including literature, may be understood as parts of a system of signs. Derrida did not believe that structuralists could explain the laws governing human signification and thus provide the key to understanding the form and meaning of everything from an African village to Greek myth to a literary text. He also rejected the structuralist belief that texts have identifiable "centres" of meaning–a belief structuralists shared with formalists.

Formalist critics, such as the New Critics, assume that a work of literature is a freestanding, self-contained object whose meaning can be found in the complex network of relations between its parts (allusions, images, rhythms, sounds, etc.). Deconstructionists, by contrast, see works in terms of their undecidability. They reject the formalist view that a work of literature is demonstrably unified from beginning to end, in one certain way, or that it is organized around a single centre that ultimately can be identified. As a result, deconstructionists see texts as more radically heterogeneous than do formalists. Formalists ultimately make sense of the ambiguities they find in a given text, arguing that every ambiguity serves a definite, meaningful, and demonstrable literary function. Undecidability, by contrast, is never reduced, let alone mastered in deconsctruction. Though a deconstructive reading can reveal the incompatible possibilities generated by the text, it is impossible for the reader to settle on any permanent meanings.

Deconstruction is a poststructuralist theory, based largely but not exclusively on the writings of Derrida. It is in the first instance a philosophical theory and a theory directed towards the (re)reading of philosophical writings. Its impact on literature, mediated in North America largely through the influences of theorists at Yale University, is based

1. On the fact that deconstruction sees all writing as a complex historical, cultural process rooted in the relations of texts to each other and in the institutions and conventions of writing, and
2. On the sophistication and intensity of its sense that human knowledge is not as controllable or as convincing as Western thought would have it and that language operates in subtle and often contradictory ways, so that certainty will always elude us.

XXXI

Death of the Author by Roland Barthes

Scan for the video

Roalnd Barthe

Q. 1 Write a critical note on "The Death of Author".
Or
Comment on the implication of "The Death of the Author" by Roland Barthes.
Ans.
Introduction:
"The Death of The Author" is 1968 essay by the French literary critic and theorist Roalnd Barthe.

In this essay, he argues against traditional literary criticism's practice of reading, which analyses a literary text on the basis of biographical context of an author and instead argues that writing and creator are unrelated.

Barthes argument in the essay:

Barthes main argument in this essay is that, it is irrelevant to interpret text based on biographical information about the author, it imposes limits upon the text.

Main idea:

- Generally, the term author means a person who writes, but Roland Barthes essay "The Death of the Author", however demonstrates that – An author is not simply a person, but a socially and historically constituted subject.

- Through this essay one can find the ideas that Barthes brings out ton relate author, language, text and reader.
- In this essay, he takes different stands through which he announces the metamorphic death of author.
- He argues that when the author writes the text his voice is no more dominant in it. How the reader interprets the text is more important.
- According to Barthes, the intentions of author is irrelevant. The work is not a replica of author's intention and in the process of giving word to the thoughts, writer intentionally or unintentionally is involved in the process of meaning making, on which he has written, there is no guarantee that author was successfully able to depict that in his work.
- But it not necessary failure of author infect it adds beauty to the text due to various possible interpretation that it might offer.
- As the writer begins, the author starts entering to his own death. It is not writer who speaks in the text, but it is the language that do so.
- Pointing towards another idea in the essays he says....Linguistically author is nothing, hence it is the language that functions.
- As soon as the author starts writings, he is dead because when he writes, he has no control over the text, rather it depends on the interpretation of reader.
- An author is one who just holds the language and has no authority over the text and meaning. It encourages the reader for interpreting any text the way he likes.

Conclusion:

The main idea of the essay "The Death of the Author is that Barthes questions the authority of the author and gives more importance to language, text and reader.

XXXII

From work to text by Roland Barthe

Scan for the video

Q.1 How does Roland Barthes differentiate a 'Work' from a 'Text'?
Or
State Roland Barthes 'ideas on 'work' and 'text' in his essay 'From to Text'.
Ans.
Introduction:
Roland Barthes is a contemporary pioneer literary critic, writer, sociologist, philosopher in French. In his article From work to text, Barthes puts forward an epoch-making theory of the Text. He distinguishes the work

and the text, denies the authority of the author and gives the reader the right to reproduce; he affirms the Text is a dynamic, open system and tries to construct a Text utopia. The post-structuralism theory of Barthes and other French philosophers as Foucault, Derrida, Lacan and Leotta was contributed to art history from 1970s.

The Essay Explained: "From Work to Text"

In his essay, From Work to Text, Barthes argues that the relation of writer, reader and observer is changed by movement from work to text. In this light, we can observe Barthes's propositions of the differences between work and text in terms of method, genres, signs, plurality, filiation, reading, and pleasure.

First of all, Barthes said that the text should not be thought as an object that can be computed. It would be futile to try to separate out materially works from texts.

Method: Barthes thought that the Text is a "methodological field" rather than a portion of the space of books", that is the work. Like Lacan's distinction between "reality" and "real": the one is displayed, the other is demonstrated. Likewise, the work can be seen and held in hand while the text is a process of demonstration, which is held in language. "The text is experienced only in an activity of production": the text is writable through tracing the flickering of presence and absence of the chain of signifiers. So, the text "cannot stop" because the process of language does not come to an end, the meaning is always suspended, something deferred or still to come.

Genre: The different genres that define the various kinds of language-narratives like biography, poetry, fiction, drama, history etc. help in creating the essentialist character of the work. The genre identifications essentialize the meanings of the language- narratives. When we approach a language-narrative, a literary piece, as a text then the genre boundaries do not work. There is the poetic nature of history, or the historic function of poetry. The text intermingles with every kinds of text, defying neat divisions that traditionally name the text. Textuality itself is the characteristic that every text shares, that defines the nature and function of all texts - history, mythology, literature, etc. All are texts, defined by their textuality. The same literature when studied with

genre divisions become the work, and with the erasure of genre boundaries, the text.

The Sign: "Whereas the Text is approached and experienced in relation to the sign, the work closes itself on a signified." Literature conceived as text can be interpreted the way a language sign is interpreted. Which means, a sign= signifier+signified. The relationship between the signifier and the signified (word and its meaning) is arbitrary and conventional. If the user community gives another meaning to the word, that meaning will become THE MEANING of the word. This principle can be amplified to understand the meanings of the texts. The words have the meanings that the community decides to give them. Which community has the power to give meanings to the language? The community that has the power to use and determine the meaning of language. So, the meanings of the text are fluid, in flux; concretized only by the users. When the literature is approached from the perspective of WORK, then the meaning is fixed, or mysterious/ambiguous. In any case the nature of the meaning is that it has essence, value, power, universality etc. It has permanence.

Plurality: The TEXT has plural meanings, the WORK singular. A literary TEXT is open to interpretations, a WORK closes off the interpretations.

Every context will create its own meaning for the text, but even within a given context , the meaning is irreducibly plural. So , in a text many meanings co-exist and each of these meanings is traversed by the others -constituting a part of it and constituted by it in turn each carrying the traces of others and inextricably linked to them.

Filiations: A WORK is studied in terms of its relations to the society, history, and the author. These three factors contribute to the essentialization of the WORK. A TEXT is independent of the authorial affiliations. Conceived in terms of TEXT, literature is free from the delimiting factors of author's motives and intentions, the text exists only as a language-construct.

Reading: The WORK is 'consumed' by the reader in the sense that the reader passively receives the meanings that literature supposedly gives. On the other hand, when literature is read like a TEXT, the reader is critically engaged with the text to the extent that he actively participates in the meaning making processes. The reader becomes the co-author of the text.

Pleasure: Literary works afford us pleasure, which is generally called aesthetic pleasure. Both the form and the content, function as organic whole. All the parts, all the constituents, are arranged in way that they become artistic creations, affording pleasure through its form as well as content. But the pleasure we receive from the work is the pleasure of consumption. This pleasure, Barthes says , is one of separation . It is linked to the fact that I cannot write what I am reading. The text on the other hand, yields a different kind of pleasure without separation.

Instead, the reader is going to be continuously implicated in producing the meaning that the text approaches. This yields a different kind of pleasure designated by Barthes and Demda by the French term 'jouissance'. We may refers to it as bliss but there is also an erotic element associated with it.

XXXIII

The Study of Poetry by Mathew Arnold

Scan for the video

Introduction:

'A Study of Poetry' is a critical essay by Matthew Arnold. Mathew Arnold is considered as one of the most significant writers of the late Victorian period in England. He established his reputation as a poet with his poems such as "The Scholar-Gypsy" and "Dover Beach". Arnold is also considered as an outstanding prose writer as his prose writings asserted his influence on literature. His writings on the role of literary criticism in society highlight the classical ideals and advocate the adoption of universal aesthetic standards. In the essay 'The Study of Poetry' Arnold criticizes the art of poetry as well as the art of criticism. Arnold believes that the art of poetry is capable of high destinies. It is the art in which the idea itself is the fact.

Analysis of essay:

1) Arnold says that we should understand the worth of poetry as it is poetry that shows us a mirror of life. Science, according to Arnold, is incomplete without poetry, and, religion and philosophy will give way to poetry. Arnold terms poetry as a criticism of life thereby refuting the accusation of Plato and says that as time goes on man will continue to find comfort and solace in poetry.

2) **Real estimate, Historic estimate and Personal estimate:** He says that when one reads poetry he tends to estimate whether it is of the best form or not. It happens in three ways- the real estimate, the historic estimate, and the personal estimate.

- **The real estimate** is an unbiased viewpoint that takes into account both the historical context and the creative faculty to judge the worth of poetry. But the real estimate is often surpassed by the historic and personal estimate. The historic estimate places the historical context above the value of the art itself. The personal estimate on the other hand depends on the personal taste, the likes and dislikes of the reader which affects his judgment of poetry. Arnold says that both these estimates tend to be fallacious.
- **Historic estimate** raises poetry to a high pedestal and thus hinders one from noticing its weaknesses. The study of the historical background of poetry and its development often leads to the critic skipping over the shortcomings because of its historical significance.
- **Personal estimate:** It is also fallacious estimate that deals with the contemporary (modern) poets. Our personal affinities, likings and circumstances have great power to sway our estimate. Due to our personal likings, we give more importance to that poetry which does not deserve that much importance. So, second fallacy in our poetic judgement is caused by personal estimate.

Thus, the real estimate is an unbiased viewpoint that takes into account both the historical context and the creative faculty to judge the worth of poetry. But the real estimate is often surpassed by the historic and personal estimate. The historic estimate places the historical context above the value of the art itself. The personal estimate on the other hand depends on the personal taste, the likes and dislikes of the reader which affects his judgment of poetry. Arnold says that both these estimates tend to be fallacious.

1. **Touchstone Method for Evaluating Poetry:** Arnold proposes the 'touchstone' method of analyzing poetry in order to determine whether it is of a high standard or not. He borrows this method from Longinus who said in his idea of the sublime that if a certain example of sublimity can please anyone regardless of habits, tastes or age and can please at all times then it can be considered as a true example of the sublime.

Arnold applies the touchstone method by taking examples from the time-tested classics and comparing them with other poetry to determine whether they possess the high poetic standard of the classics.

Arnold quotes Homer, Dante, Shakespeare and Milton in an attempt to exemplify touchstone poetry. He says that the examples he has quoted are very dissimilar to one another but they all possess a high poetic quality.

1. **Analysis of the English Classics**

Arnold then highlights the impact of French poets (especially from Northern France) on their English counterparts. However, their poetry was dominated by romance over serious and graver themes of human life.

Arnold is full of praise for Chaucer who he believes wrote in 'liquid diction' and was a great exponent of both content and style. According to Arnold, Chaucer scores high on the real estimate but does not come to the level of a classical poet lacking seriousness of someone like Dante, Milton, and Shakespeare who all are classical poets.

3. **Continuity of the Classics**

Arnold claims since the classics works have been able to stand the test of time and longevity they have an indwelling ability of self-conservation. This ability is a function of the self-preserving and enduring nature of human beings.

According to Arnold, human nature remains consistent through various epochs and times and since the classics deal with the topics and issues highlighting and commenting on human suffering, emotions, and nature.

As long as they stimulate such emotions and thoughts in the readers that will remain alive in their hearts and minds.

Conclusion:

Arnold concludes the essay by pointing out that one is on dangerous ground when one approaches the poetry of poets who are near to one in time because the personal estimate is bound to influence one's clear judgement. But it is possible to overcome this danger by using the touchstone method. The real estimate would benefit the reader by helping him to feel clearly and enjoy deeply the best and the classic in poetry.

XXXIV

"THE FUNCTION OF CRITICISM" by Matthew Arnold

scan for the video

Mathew Arnold

Introduction:

Mathew Arnold is considered as one of the most significant writers of the late Victorian period in England. He established his reputation as a poet with his poems such as "The Scholar-Gypsy" and "Dover Beach". Matthew Arnold's other essay, "The Function of Criticism at Present Time," written thirteen years after the preface, is an essay in which Arnold dwells on a critic's responsibility to the reading public. His work goes beyond a narrow interpretation of the judgment of works of art and embraces a more extensive range.

Definition of criticism by Arnold

"The Function of Criticism in the Present Time is largely made of ideas that Arnold discusses in his Study of Poetry. He defines criticism as "A disinterested endeavor to learn and propagate the best that is known and thought of in the world, and thus to establish a current of fresh and true ideas." The term 'disinterest' in the view of Arnold refers to being an impartial and just reader. A critic needs to be free from two prejudices: historical and personal. Historical prejudice is when the critic resorts to view through the lens of past and neglects the present in the work. Personal prejudice refers to a personal liking that can cloud judgment.

Arnold also believes that for the production of great literary work, the 'power of man' and 'power of the moment' must come together. If one of them is absent, the work will not become great. To illustrate this, he takes the example of Goethe and Byron. Both had great productive power, yet Goethe's work was more powerful because he had a rich cultural background. He also mentions how Shakespeare was not a deep reader, which affected his work. But his fame and glory were a result of his age and a climate of great ideas.

Three functions for the critic

By the definition of criticism provided by Arnold, the task of a critic is threefold.

The first task is the critic's duty to learn, and for that he must "see things as they really are".

The second task is to hand on this idea to others, to convert the world, to make "the best ideas prevail."

The third task requires the critic to create a favorable atmosphere for the creative genius of the future, by promoting "a current of ideas in the highest degree animating and nourishing to the creative power." Without the prevalence of best ideas, there will be a cultural anarchy.

Arnold also observes that to recognize the greatness of a literary work, one has to look beyond the social ideas and influences that cast shadows and opinions. Further, he indicates that two powers must converge to create a great piece of literature: the power of man and the power of moment. In the quest to be a critic, Arnold believed that one must not confine himself to the literature if his own country, but should draw substantially on foreign literature and ideas because the propagation of ideas should be an objective endeavor. Scott-James says that Arnold places the critic "is the position of John the Baptist, preparing the ways for one whose shoe he is not worthy to unloose". Thus, Arnold has a high conception of the vocation of a critic.

Role of Criticism

Arnold suggests that the function of criticism at the present time is to make itself inherently valuable in itself. Whether the value springs from bringing joy to the writer or from making sure that the best ideas reach society are irrespective. In this regard, Arnold mirrors Aristotle's view of poetry while he explains that the highest function of human kind is exercising its creative power.

Criticism performs another important function as well. It rouses men out of their self-satisfaction and complacency. By shaking complacency off, criticism makes their mind dwell upon what is excellent in itself, and makes them contemplate the ideally perfect. Therefore, the critic must rise above practical considerations and have ideal perfection as his aim, in order to make others rise to it as well.

Defence on Significance of Criticism

Arnold argues that a lot of literature from European nations has been used for the purpose of criticism. But England has failed to produce and encourage significant amount of critical writing due to the attitudes of writers towards criticism. He takes the example of Wordsworth to illustrate this further. Wordsworth believed that critical writing was a waste of time for the author as well as the reader. He also states that great harm can be done through critical writing, but little harm occurs through means of creative writing. But Arnold defends these views by arguing that if a man has talent in one line of writing, he must not be forced to create original writing under the pretext that critical writing is of no value. To quote,

"It is almost too much to expect a poor human nature, that a man capable of producing some effect in one line of literature, should for the greater good of society, voluntarily doom himself to impotence and obscurity in another."

Arnold goes on to point out the paradox of Wordsworth's beliefs on criticism as Wordsworth had indulged himself in being a critic by writing against literary criticism.

Literary Criticism and Creativity: Arnold believed creative capacity to be more important than critical faculty.

However, his definition of criticism as "the endeavor, in all branches of knowledge, theology, philosophy, history, art, science, to see the object as in itself it really is" makes it a necessary prerequisite for valuable creation. He asserts that creation of quality is not possible if people are not provided with a current of fresh ideas. This is achieved through honest criticism. If the best ideas do not prevail, it gives rise to a cultural anarchy. Only when the power of man and power of moment come together can a good piece of literature be created.

Arnold also states that writing criticism may produce in its practitioner a sense of creative joy. He compares the emotional state of writing criticism with the emotional state of creative writing. In this, he dispels the typical censure that criticism serves no purpose.

Arnold observes that great writing emerges from great ideas, and they are manifested when these ideas reach the masses. The critic performs the important task of identifying these ideas with disinterest and impart these ideas to people. He implies that the period of great creativity and dormant creativity can be traced to lack of objective criticism and public attention as much as to creators of great work. In this argument, Arnold establishes literary criticism as an art form as high and significant as any form of creativity.

Further, Arnold argues that critical writing is an important activity of exercising free creativity. "It is undeniable, also, that men may have the sense of exercising this free creative activity in other ways than in producing great works of literature or art." If some people were better equipped to write criticism, it would be frustrating to insist they channel their talent only for creating original writing.

Finally, criticism is necessary because Arnold thinks that creative power works with certain materials, and for the author these ideas, "the best ideas on every matter which literature touch, current at the time." However, authors do not discover these ideas, rather they synthesize them into their work of art. Therefore, if authors do not readily know these ideas, they have nothing to write about. Arnold talks about the power of man and power of the moment, in this context. The author needs to live in a society where true ideas are discussed and debated, where true thoughts are cherished and passed on, like in ancient Greece or Renaissance England. Thus he advocates that good criticism propagates good literature.

Conclusion:

Matthew Arnold is hailed as the first 'modern critic' and is also called a 'critic's critic' for his contribution to the meaningfulness of criticism in the realm of literature. In his work 'The Function of Criticism at the Present Time' (1865), Arnold makes an effort to demonstrate that criticism in itself has several functions and should be observed as an art form that is as high and important as any other creative art form. He offered an objective method in the field of criticism, through comparison and analysis. His methods were met with disapproval from his peers. However, Arnold's method for literary criticism was widely accepted and went on to influence the first sixty years of the 20thcentury. Arnold has a high conception of the vocation of a critic and the function of criticism. His ideas are a result of the prevalence of cultural anarchy, leading him to take up the mission to bring about cultural regeneration in the literary world through means of objective criticism. His critic is a critic of life, society, religion culture, national character and all aesthetic activities

Previous years Question Papers

XXXV
Question paper 1

Time : 3 hours Maximum Marks : 100

Note : Answer any five of the following questions in your own words as far as possible.

1. Comment on Plato's views on poetry. 20

2. Attempt a critique of Romanticism. 20

3. "Honest criticism and sensitive appreciation are directed not upon the poet but upon the poetry." Comment. 20

4. How do Marxists understand literature ? Support your points with suitable examples. 20

5. Assess the contribution of Mary Wollstonecraft to the emancipation of women. 20

6. Evaluate either Freud's or Lacan's contribution to the understanding of literature. 20

7. Write short notes on any two of the following : 20

(a) Rasa

(b) Aucitya

(c) Hamartia

(d) Death of the Author

(e) Matthew Arnold as a Critic

XXXVI

Question paper 2

MEG-05

MASTER'S DEGREE PROGRAMME IN

ENGLISH

Tenn-End Examination June, 2020

MEG-05 : LITERARY CRITICISM AND THEORY

Time : 3 Hours Maximum Marks : 100

Note : Answer Question No. 1 and any other four of the remaining questions. Each question carries 20 marks.

1. Write short notes on any two of the following (200 words): 10x2=20

(a) Structuralism

(b) Poetry as inspiration

(c) Fancy and Imagination

(d) Simone De Beauvoir

2. Literary criticism has a social function. Discuss. 20

3. Explain in your own words Aristotle's theory of mimesis. 20

4. Briefly explain 'The intentional fallacy' and `The affective fallacy'. 20

5. What is meant by 'superstructure' in Marxist Theory? How would you interpret it? 20

6. What is meant by the death of the author in critical theory? 20

7. Attempt a critique of post-colonial theory with special reference to Said, Spivak and Bhabha. 20

XXXVII
Question Paper 3

December, 2019

MEG-5 : LITERARY CRITICISM AND THEORY

Time : 3 hours Maximum Marks : 100

<u>*Note : Answer any five of the following questions. Each question carries 20 marks.*</u>

1. Explain how Plato views art as twice removed from reality. 20

2. Attempt a critique of 'Rasa' as understood in ancient Indian literature. 20

3. Critically examine S.T. Coleridge's views on the esemplastic power of the poetic imagination. 20

4. 'New criticism' emphasizes the text, not the background. Comment. 20

5. What is superstructure in Marxist criticism ? Provide examples of superstructures. How do they function ? 20

6. Evaluate Elaine Showalter's contribution to feminist criticism. 20

7. Analyse John Donne's The Canonization' with the tools of 'Deconstruction'. 20

8. What does Spivak mean by `Subalternity'? Explain with examples. 20

XXXVIII

Question Paper 4

MASTER'S DEGREE PROGRAMME IN ENGLISH
Term-End Examination
June, 2019
MEG-005 : LITERARY CRITICISM AND THEORY

Time : 3 hours Maximum Marks : 100

Note : Answer any five of the following questions. Each question carries 20 marks.

1. Explain how Aristotle argues in favour of "drama as a larger and higher form of art".

2. Give an account of Sphota theory as explained by Sanskrit theoreticians.

3. Critically examine Wordsworth's view that "all good poetry is the spontaneous overflow of powerful feelings".

4. What according to John Crowe Ransom is the role of the literary critic in the modern world ? Explain.

5. Attempt a short essay on the relation between literature and ideology.

6. 'From the tyranny of man... the greater number of female follies proceed.' In the light of this statement evaluate Mary Wollstonecraft's thoughts on women.

7. How does Roland Barthes differentiate a 'Work' from a 'Text' ? Explain in your own words.

8. What are Foucault's views on discourse and power ? Explain.

XXXIX

Question Paper 5

MASTER'S DEGREE PROGRAMME
IN ENGLISH
Term-End Examination
June, 2018
MEG-5 : LITERARY CRITICISM AND THEORY

Time : 3 hours Maximum Marks : 100

Note : Answer any five of the following questions. All questions carry equal marks.

1. Write short notes on any two of the following : 2x10=20

(a) On the Sublime

(b) Mikhail Bakhtin

(c) Deconstruction

(d) Resistance to Theory

(e) Rasa

2. Enumerate the six elements of tragedy according to Aristotle and explain any two of them with suitable examples. 20

3. Briefly outline Wordsworth's theory of poetic diction with special reference to the 'Preface' to the Lyrical Ballads. 20

4. Bring out the features of New Criticism. 20

5. Explain in your own words Marx's views of the base — superstructure relationship. How does an artist become conscious of it in his/her creations ? 20

6. State Roland Barthes' ideas on 'work' and 'text' in his essay 'From Work to Text'. 20

7. What are the major concerns of postcolonial theorists ? 20

XL
Question Paper 6

MASTER'S DEGREE PROGRAMME
IN ENGLISH
Term-End Examination
December, 2018

MEG-5 : LITERARY CRITICISM AND THEORY

Time : 3 hours Maximum Marks : 100

Note : Answer any five of the following questions. All questions carry equal marks.

1. Write short notes on any two of the following : 2x10=20

(a) Signifier and Signified

(b) Apology for Poetry

(c) Structuralism

(d) Russian Formalists

(e) Dhvani

2. Discuss 'mimesis' in the light of Plato and Aristotle's postulations. 20

3. Romantics assert that "imagination transcends reason". Discuss. 20

4. Evaluate I.A. Richards's contribution to literary criticism. 20

5. Discuss the major concerns of feminist theory. 20

6. Examine how Waiting for Godot problematizes the meaninglessness of life. 20

7. Attempt a critique of Midnight's Children as a postmodernist text. 20

XLI

Question Paper 7

MASTER'S DEGREE PROGRAMME
IN ENGLISH
Term-End Examination
June, 2017
MEG-5 : LITERARY CRITICISM AND THEORY

Time : 3 hours Maximum Marks : 100

Note : Answer any five of the following questions.

1. Discuss Aristotle's view of the plot in tragedy. 20

2. What role does Shelley assign to poets in the nineteenth century ? Explain. 20

3. What according to John Crowe Ransom are the "duties" of a critic ? Explain. 20

4. Explain with the help of suitable examples, the Marxian concept of base and superstructure. 20

5. Evaluate Elaine Showalter's contribution to feminist criticism. 20

6. What according to Barthes is the difference between 'work' and 'text'? Explain. 20

7. Briefly introduce two major post-colonial critics and their contribution to our understanding of literature. 20

8. Write short notes on any two of the following: 2 x10=20

(a) Signifier

(b) Irony

(c) Alamkara

(d) Rasa

XLII

Question Paper 8

MASTER'S DEGREE PROGRAMME
IN ENGLISH
Term-End Examination
December, 2017
MEG-5 : LITERARY CRITICISM AND THEORY

Time : 3 hours Maximum Marks : 100

Note : Answer any five questions. All questions carry equal marks.

1. Why does Plato declare the role of the poet as subversive ? 20

2. What does Wordsworth think of the distinction between the language of prose and metrical composition ? 20

3. Write short notes on any two of the following : 2x10=20

(a) Tragic Hero

(b) Hamartia

(c) Sphota

(d) Alamkara

(e) Sruti

(f) Objective Correlative

4. Discuss the ideas expressed by Cleanth Brooks in his essay "Irony as a Principle of Structure". 20

5. Write a critical note on the essentials of Marxist literary theory OR Freudian psychoanalysis. 20

6. Comment on the significance of the title The Second Sex. 20

7. Why does Derrida resist definitions ? Give reasons for your answer. 20

8. What is Raymond Williams' contribution to Cultural Studies ? 20

XLIII
Question Paper 9

MASTER'S DEGREE PROGRAMME
IN ENGLISH
Term-End Examination
December, 2016
MEG-5 : LITERARY CRITICISM AND THEORY

Time : 3 hours Maximum Marks : 100

Note : Answer any five of the following questions. All questions carry equal marks.

1. Write a critical note on Aristotle's concept of tragedy. 20

2. Evaluate Wordsworth's 'Preface' to the Lyrical Ballads (1800) as, an attack on the "inane

phraseology" of many 18thcentury writers. 20

3. The 'truth which the poet utters' according to Cleanth Brooks, 'can be approached only in terms of paradox'. Do you agree ? Supply reasons for your answer. 20

4. Explain Marx's idea of dialectical materialism. How does it help us in understanding literature ? 20

5. Assess Mary Wollstonecraft's contribution to Women's rights and their education. 20

6. Comment on the implications of The Death of the Author' by Roland Barthes. 20

7. How are 'lack' and 'desire' closely connected in Lacan's theory ? 20

8. Write short notes on any two of the following : 2x10=20

(a) Sruti

(b) Dhvani

(c) Mimesis

(d) Paradox

XLIV

Question Paper 10

MASTER'S DEGREE PROGRAMME
IN ENGLISH
Term-End Examination
June, 2015
MEG-5 : LITERARY CRITICISM AND THEORY

Time : 3 hours Maximum Marks : 100

Note : Question no. 1 is compulsory. Attempt any four from the remaining questions. All questions carry equal marks.

I. Write short notes on any two of the following : 10+10

(a) Ethos

(b) Hamartia

(c) Emotions recollected in tranquillity

(d) Objective correlative

(e) Mode of production

(f) Signifier

2. Discuss Aristotle's theory of tragedy and its different elements. 20

3. In higher poetry, we look for "the wisdom of the heart and the grandeur of the imagination". Examine the statement in the context of Wordsworth's Preface to the Lyrical Ballads. 20

4. Critically examine the role of ideology in litefary production following the Marxist critical theory. 20

5. Evaluate Elain Showalter's `gynocriticism' and its value in the context of feminist criticism. 20

6. What is 'deconstruction' ? Is 'deconstruction' an effective tool for analysing a literary text ? Give a reasoned answer. 20

7. Discuss critically the seminal issues that Post-Colonial theory addresses. 20

8. Critically examine Wimsatt's concept of "The Intentional Fallacy". 20